Nuclear Submarine Disasters

GREAT DISASTERS
REFORMS and RAMIFICATIONS

Nuclear Submarine Disasters

Christopher Higgins

CHELSEA HOUSE PUBLISHERS
Philadelphia

Frontispiece: A U.S. nuclear submarine travels along the ocean surface. Since the first nuclear submarine was launched in 1954, there have been a number of underwater catastrophes, often resulting in the loss of entire vessels and their crews.

Dedication: To my wife, Sima; thanks for putting up with seven months of submarines.

CHELSEA HOUSE PUBLISHERS

Editor in Chief Sally Cheney
Associate Editor in Chief Kim Shinners
Production Manager Pamela Loos
Art Director Sara Davis
Production Editor Diann Grasse

Staff for NUCLEAR SUBMARINE DISASTERS

Senior Editor LeeAnne Gelletly
Associate Art Director/Designer Takeshi Takahashi
Layout 21st Century Publishing and Communications, Inc.

First Printing

1 3 5 7 9 8 6 4 2

The Chelsea House World Wide Web address is
http://www.chelseahouse.com

Library of Congress Cataloging-in-Publication Data

Higgins, Chris.
     Nuclear submarine disasters / Chris Higgins.
          p. cm. — (Great disasters, reforms and ramifications)
     Summary: Presents a history of disasters involving nuclear submarines, including the Thresher, the Scorpion, and the Kursk, and explores how the investigation of these accidents can lead to safety reform.
     ISBN 0-7910-6329-1 (alk. paper)
       1. Nuclear submarines—Accidents—Juvenile literature.
[1. Nuclear submarines—Accidents.] I. Title. II. Series.

V857.5 .H54 2001
910.4'52—dc21
                                                            2001047238

Contents

GREAT DISASTERS
REFORMS and RAMIFICATIONS

Jill McCaffrey
National Chairman
Armed Forces Emergency Services
American Red Cross

Introduction

Disasters have always been a source of fascination and awe. Tales of a great flood that nearly wipes out all life are among humanity's oldest recorded stories, dating at least from the second millennium B.C., and they appear in cultures from the Middle East to the Arctic Circle to the southernmost tip of South America and the islands of Polynesia. Typically gods are at the center of these ancient disaster tales—which is perhaps not too surprising, given the fact that the tales originated during a time when human beings were at the mercy of natural forces they did not understand.

To a great extent, we still are at the mercy of nature, as anyone who reads the newspapers or watches nightly news broadcasts can attest.

Hurricanes, earthquakes, tornados, wildfires, and floods continue to exact a heavy toll in suffering and death, despite our considerable knowledge of the workings of the physical world. If science has offered only limited protection from the consequences of natural disasters, it has in no way diminished our fascination with them. Perhaps that's because the scale and power of natural disasters force us as individuals to confront our relatively insignificant place in the physical world and remind us of the fragility and transience of our lives. Perhaps it's because we can imagine ourselves in the midst of dire circumstances and wonder how we would respond. Perhaps it's because disasters seem to bring out the best and worst instincts of humanity: altruism and selfishness, courage and cowardice, generosity and greed.

As one of the national chairmen of the American Red Cross, a humanitarian organization that provides relief for victims of disasters, I have had the privilege of seeing some of humanity's best instincts. I have witnessed communities pulling together in the face of trauma; I have seen thousands of people answer the call to help total strangers in their time of need.

Of course, helping victims after a tragedy is not the only way, or even the best way, to deal with disaster. In many cases planning and preparation can minimize damage and loss of life—or even avoid a disaster entirely. For, as history repeatedly shows, many disasters are caused not by nature but by human folly, shortsightedness, and unethical conduct. For example, when a land developer wanted to create a lake for his exclusive resort club in Pennsylvania's Allegheny Mountains in 1880, he ignored expert warnings and cut corners in reconstructing an earthen dam. On May 31, 1889, the dam gave way, unleashing 20 million tons of water on the towns below. The Johnstown Flood, the deadliest in American history, claimed more than 2,200 lives. Greed and negligence would figure prominently in the Triangle Shirtwaist Company fire in 1911. Deplorable conditions in the garment sweatshop, along with a failure to give any thought to the safety of workers, led to the tragic deaths of 146 persons. Technology outstripped wisdom only a year later, when the designers of the luxury liner *Titanic* smugly declared their state-of-the-art ship "unsinkable," seeing no need to provide lifeboat capacity for everyone onboard. On the night of April 14, 1912, more than 1,500 passengers and crew paid for this hubris with their lives after the ship collided with an iceberg and sank. But human catastrophes aren't always the unforeseen consequences of carelessness or folly. In the 1940s the leaders of Nazi Germany purposefully and systematically set out to exterminate all Jews, along with Gypsies, homosexuals, the mentally ill, and other so-called undesirables. More recently terrorists have targeted random members of society, blowing up airplanes and buildings in an effort to advance their political agendas.

The books in the GREAT DISASTERS: REFORMS AND RAMIFICATIONS series examine these and other famous disasters, natural and human made. They explain the causes of the disasters, describe in detail how events unfolded, and paint vivid portraits of the people caught up in dangerous circumstances. But these books are more than just accounts of what happened to whom and why. For they place the disasters in historical perspective, showing how people's attitudes and actions changed and detailing the steps society took in the wake of each calamity. And in the end, the most important lesson we can learn from any disaster—as well as the most fitting tribute to those who suffered and died—is how to avoid a repeat in the future.

On the Bottom

The first nuclear submarine disaster of the 21st century happened to the Russian submarine *Kursk,* seen here in a May 2000 photo taken three months before it sank to the bottom of the Barents Sea. The disaster, which took the lives of 118 sailors, received international media attention for several weeks.

We won't hold out for 24 hours.

—from a note found on the recovered body of a *Kursk* sailor

On Saturday, August 12, 2000, the Russian Northern Fleet was holding a rare 50-ship training exercise in the icy waters of the Barents Sea. Located north of Russia, far from the capital city of Moscow, the Barents Sea adjoins the Scandinavian Peninsula containing Finland, Sweden, and Norway. A cold and unforgiving place, the sea is home to numerous Northern Fleet submarines and surface-ship bases. Patrolling and training in these Arctic Circle waters has been a part of Russian defense strategy for generations.

The United States and its North Atlantic Treaty Organization (NATO) allies have been there for just as long, observing every Russian move and developing their own naval defense strategies and tactics. In the event of war, Russian naval forces based in the Barents Sea would move into the Atlantic Ocean. With the information that they gathered from spying on the Russian vessels during their training exercises, the United States and NATO would have a wartime edge.

The August training exercises were the biggest in some time for Russia because of budget constraints. The previous 10 years had been very difficult economically for the new government. Many Russian institutions and citizens had found it hard to make ends meet in the years since the end of the cold war in 1990, with the subsequent fall of communism and transition to a capitalist economy. The Russian military had to cope with budget cuts, equipment shortages, low pay, a stubborn guerrilla war in Chechnya, and an erosion of the quality of its soldiers. Under communism, professional soldiers had comprised the Russian military, but entering the 21st century, it was largely made up of conscripts: soldiers who are drafted into service rather than voluntarily joining the military. Today's typical Russian conscripts are high school–aged men who are given uniforms and receive what amounts to basic on-the-job training.

That summer day, doubts about military competence were probably not distracting the crew of the massive submarine K-149, SSGN *Kursk,* the pride of the Russian submarine fleet. SSGN is a military classification that is an acronym for *S*ubmersible *S*hip carrying *G*uided missiles and powered by a *N*uclear reactor. NATO classifies ships of all navies as well, and it classified the *Kursk* as an Oscar 2–class submarine. Powered by two nuclear reactors, *Kursk* weighed almost 14,000 tons and could travel at a top speed of 28 knots submerged and 15 knots on the surface.

Named for the location of one of the most decisive battles against the Germans during World War II, *Kursk* was one of the newest ships in Russia's submarine fleet, launched in 1995. The people of the city of Kursk looked to the namesake vessel with pride and lovingly sent their sons to serve aboard the submarine. They also sent food. In times of both peace and war, submariners have one of the most dangerous jobs in the world, and navies acknowledge this by providing sub crews with the best food possible. Since Russia's budget crunch had cut down on the amount of food available to the navy, civilian families of crewmen often stepped in to fill the gap.

Kursk was more than one and a half football fields in length at the keel, or bottom, and about half the width of a football field at the beam. It was built with a double hull that was robust enough to withstand a torpedo attack from its natural enemy, an American Los Angeles–class nuclear-attack submarine. In the event of war, the double hull would give *Kursk* a chance to complete its primary mission: Sink an enemy aircraft carrier and as much of the carrier's task force as possible.

On the morning of August 12, *Kursk* was test-firing torpedoes and participating in training exercises in conjunction with other ships. American, British, and Norwegian submarines and surface ships were in the area monitoring the activities. *Kursk* was probably carrying its full complement of 24 cruise missiles plus 28 torpedoes and perhaps a few mines, as well. According to various news reports, it was not carrying any nuclear warheads. At 505 feet long, 59 feet wide, and 29 feet high, *Kursk* had more than enough room to pack on board all of its potent weapons and its crew of 113, plus 5 extra observers for a total of 118.

Kursk had completed one torpedo launch that day and was preparing to fire another salvo. Captain Gennadi Lyachin brought the vessel to a periscope depth of approximately 60 feet. He probably looked for a target by peering through the scope, then ordered his crew to prepare to fire the weapon.

The executive officer would have taken over from there. He and other members of the control room weapons crew would have fed information on the target's location into computers, which would have come up with a "solution," or compass bearing indicating the direction that the torpedo should travel and its proper depth and speed. (The term *solution* refers to the answer to the complicated geometry problem that crewmen face: how to hit a moving or stationary target on or beneath the surface from a submarine that may also be moving from a location on or beneath the surface.) After the weapons crew entered the solution information into the computers controlling the torpedo, they would confirm the settings, and the executive officer would then inform Captain Lyachin that the weapon was ready to fire.

It is uncertain whether Captain Lyachin ever heard the words "Solution set, Captain," indicating that the torpedo was ready. Suddenly, at 11:28:27 A.M., an explosion tore through the torpedo room in the bow, or front, of the submarine. Captain Lyachin did not send an SOS or launch the emergency beacon. In fact, nothing was ever heard from *Kursk*.

After the explosion, the sub began a slow descent, angling down at the bow, toward the bottom of the Barents Sea. It is likely that the underwater explosion killed or injured many men in the forward spaces of the ship. Survivors would have immediately emptied the water from the vessel's ballast tanks to try to bring the submarine to the surface. (Ballast, or weight, allows the submarine to dive;

when ballast tanks are emptied, compressed air replaces the water, making the vessel buoyant.)

Flames probably broke out immediately inside the sub and water began pouring into the torpedo room through cracked piping or through a breach in the seal of the torpedo room escape hatch. The Russian crew would have quickly donned emergency gear: protective clothing and masks to help the men breathe while fighting the heat, smoke, and toxic gases of a fire.

Because fire presents a huge and especially difficult problem aboard a submarine, all submariners undergo extensive training to fight such catastrophes. A submariner cannot, of course, just open a hatch and jump overboard if all is lost—opening a hatch beneath the

Gennadi Lyachin, commander of the *Kursk*, salutes other Russian officials upon returning from a trip to the Mediterranean Sea in October 1999. The following year, Lyachin, along with the rest of his crew, died in the *Kursk* disaster.

A Russian technician inspects a torpedo on board a nuclear submarine of the Oscar class, the same class to which the *Kursk* belonged. An explosion in the torpedo room of the *Kursk* sent the submarine 350 feet to the sea floor below.

surface would doom the occupants of a sub to drowning. And a fire can quickly use up the limited supply of oxygen, causing death by asphyxiation or smoke inhalation for the submariners. Furthermore, if fire occurs in a crucial component of a sub, it could prevent the vessel from rising. Although the crew could survive a soft landing on a sandy sea floor, rescue in such a situation could occur only in shallow coastal waters—and most of the time submarines travel in stretches of the ocean where ocean depth is measured in miles, not feet. Water pressure would eventually crush a sinking submarine flat if it descended beyond what is known as its crush depth. Most nuclear subs have a crush depth of between 700 and 3000 feet.

A fire requires a quick response and an emergency trip to the surface. If a fire did break out on *Kursk*, it probably grew larger when a second explosion occurred two minutes later. In Norway, seismologists—technicians who normally record the vibrations of earthquakes—registered an explosion that day in the Barents Sea measuring 3.5 on the Richter scale—the size of a small earthquake. (U.S., British, and Norwegian ships in the area also noted the two explosions. According to numerous news reports, sonar operators listening in had to tear off their headsets to avoid damaging their ears because the blasts were so loud.) Scientists later theorized that this explosion had the force of about two tons of TNT and would have killed anyone still alive in the torpedo room and killed or disabled most of the men in the forward part of the ship. As divers would later discover, the explosion also blew a hole through the hull of the ship, exposing the torpedo room to the sea, and effectively ending the life of *Kursk*.

Water poured through the gaping wound of the torpedo room, drowning crewmen, drenching electronic equipment, and crunching bulkheads. Events transpired so quickly that the men had no chance to close the watertight hatches that would have sealed the breached compartment. As the ship sank deeper, water pressure increased as well, further hindering efforts to stop the influx of water. The weight of the water flowing into the ship would have counteracted any blowing of the ballast tanks.

As more water entered the ship, its downward angle increased, sinking it faster and faster as more spaces flooded. Additional equipment probably failed and more men died—drowned, burned to death, or crippled by the rising air pressure as water poured in and compressed the remaining air. After the radio space flooded, survivors would not have been able to radio emergency messages to the surface.

The control room appears to have quickly flooded, preventing anyone from using the escape pod located in the sail of the sub. Located directly above the control room, the sail, commonly called the conning tower, is the raised finlike tower above the deck of a submarine that provides the sub's familiar distinctive shape. Periscopes and many necessary antennae are fitted to the sail of a modern submarine, which is streamlined to cut through the water with no resistance. Russian submarine designers include an escape pod in the sails of their subs—and *Kursk*'s pod would have saved the entire regular crew of 113. However, disaster investigators believe that water flooded the ship all the way to the nuclear reactor space in the stern, or rear of the ship, blocking the way to the pod. In the stern, however, protective shielding meant to block radiation effectively stopped the water, allowing the sailors in the stern to survive the explosion.

Apart from the explosions and their consequences, the men in the forward spaces and control room died for yet another reason. All submariners train to save their ship, which for the military is more important than an individual life. The doomed sailors in these areas would have remained at their posts until the absolute last minute, doing everything in their power to keep *Kursk* under control and bring her back to the surface, stemming the influx of water and keeping the two nuclear reactors safely functioning.

The survivors in the stern of *Kursk* rode the submarine as it sank to the bottom. The twin propellers continued to turn, moving the ship forward as the ship plowed into the mud. The men who could have stopped them were dead at the control panels. Captain Lyachin's voice would never give the order to stop. As the sub collided

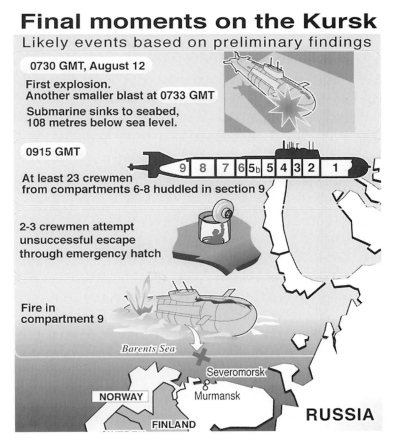

Final moments on the Kursk
Likely events based on preliminary findings

0730 GMT, August 12

First explosion.
Another smaller blast at 0733 GMT

Submarine sinks to seabed,
108 metres below sea level.

0915 GMT

At least 23 crewmen
from compartments 6-8 huddled in section 9

2-3 crewmen attempt
unsuccessful escape
through emergency hatch

Fire in
compartment 9

Barents Sea

Severomorsk

NORWAY   Murmansk

FINLAND   **RUSSIA**

Because the crew of the *Kursk* did not maintain radio contact with the surface after the two explosions occurred, the crew members' actions following the disaster—as well as its cause—have not been completely determined. This illustration shows one possible sequence of events that may have happened after the blasts.

with the sea bottom, the impact would have thrown the remaining crewmen (and loose equipment) around like toys, injuring and perhaps killing many.

The twin nuclear reactors may have functioned a while longer, providing heat, light, electricity, fresh air, and water. However, not long after *Kursk* settled onto the sea bottom, the reactors would have stopped automatically. The water needed to cool them had to be drawn from ports at the keel of the ship, so once these intakes had clogged with mud, control rods would have dropped into each radioactive core, stopping the nuclear reaction before a meltdown, or uncontrollable overheating, could occur.

Nuclear submarines rely on their reactors for power, propulsion, clean air, and fresh water. The submariners of *Kursk* were now without most of these essentials. If the ship's batteries had not been destroyed in the blast and collision with the sea floor, electricity would have lasted a little while; but after the batteries died, the only light would have come from emergency battle lanterns. Some authorities believe that *Kursk* was not even carrying any batteries due to equipment shortages.

Meanwhile, the chill of the frigid arctic waters gradually crept over the ship. The unlucky men of the stricken vessel would have waited for a rescue at 350 feet below the Barents Sea, trying to conserve air by sitting still or lying in their bunks. The sailors would have put on any clothing they could find and huddled in groups to stay warm. Any men who had managed to escape from the bow to the stern were probably soaked to the skin. Air quality would have been poor. As water leaked into the dry space, it would have compressed the remaining air and increased atmospheric pressure, causing pain in the eardrums and requiring the sailors to swallow to equalize the pressure.

As time passed, the air would have become stale with carbon dioxide (CO_2), exhaled from the men, and carbon monoxide (CO), emitted by the fire. To absorb the CO_2 from the air, the sailors would have lit special candles and spread special powders on the floor. These methods would have worked for a while, but nothing could have replenished the oxygen or gotten rid of the carbon monoxide. Eventually the air would have become so oxygen-depleted that the candles would not stay lit. At first a lack of oxygen would afflict the survivors with crushing headaches worse than any migraine. Eventually the men would loose consciousness. Finally, death would occur.

It was clear to the ships on the surface that some men

aboard *Kursk* had survived the explosion. Sonar equipment picked up tapping sounds, probably coming from someone banging a hammer on the hull. The hammering would have helped raise the morale of the survivors, giving them hope that the ships above them would hone in on the sound and rescue them; the act itself probably helped warm up the sailor doing the hammering as the temperature dropped. But as the air soured, at some point even the lightest blow of the hammer would have required superhuman strength to manage. Eventually, the sonar equipment could no longer detect any tapping.

Although they probably knew that their fate was sealed, the men of *Kursk* had no choice but to hope for rescue. They made no attempt to swim to the surface for a number of reasons. The submarine lay 350 feet down, and although it is possible in theory to make a swimming escape from a submarine (called a free escape) at this depth, in practice the odds against success rise as the depth increases.

The escape breathing equipment of the U.S. and British navies permits submariners to escape from depths of up to 500 feet. And while the Russian navy probably had the same kind of equipment, it is unlikely the *Kursk* sailors had undergone the necessary hours of practice required for a successful free escape. Such an attempt would be dangerous: if the swimmers hold their breath while ascending, their lungs would explode as the water pressure decreased on the way to the surface. Death would be instantaneous.

Another concern was "the bends," which results from a too-rapid rise to the surface. As the swimmer ascends, nitrogen, a component of air, is forced out of the bloodstream and into the body's joints and tissues. The bends will cause an excruciating level of pain, paralysis, and often death. Increased water pressure can also cause

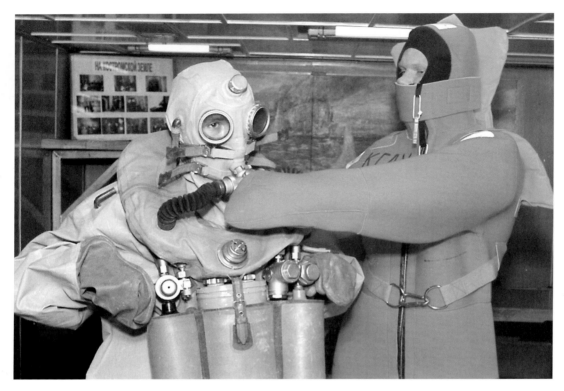

Submarine sailors train with escape suits, which crewmen can use as protection during an underwater emergency exit from the vessel. Some experts claimed that a lack of training using these suits prevented members of the *Kursk* crew from escaping from the sunken sub.

oxygen narcosis, a condition in which the oxygen breathed by the swimmer produces a dangerous drunken feeling of euphoria. This feeling can cause even the most experienced diver to make a deadly mistake he or she would never make at a more shallow depth.

The bends and oxygen narcosis are both conditions that occur in deep waters, and both require the diver to make a careful controlled ascent to the surface. Divers use a watch, a line with depth markers, and decompression chambers to combat the effects of water pressure. Some dives require hours of decompression. Therefore, even if the *Kursk* sailors could have escaped on their own and reached the surface, it is likely there would have been no decompression chamber to greet them. And with the water temperature close to freezing, even in the event of a successful ascent, they might well have frozen to death, anyway. The odds were very much against escaping from the stricken sub.

The men of *Kursk* are one crew in a long line of submarine sailors who have been killed in maritime disasters. In the past 50 years no submarines have been lost in combat, but the United States, Britain, Israel, and Russia (formerly of the USSR) have all lost at least one submarine with all hands. Men have been dying in submarines ever since a sailor closed the hatch on the first prototype and disappeared beneath the waves.

Iron Coffins, Pigboats, and FBMs

2

You like the sea, Captain?

Yes, I love it! The sea is everything. . . . In it is supreme tranquility. The sea does not belong to despots. Upon its surface men can still exercise unjust laws, fight, tear one another to pieces, and be carried away with terrestrial horrors. But at thirty feet below its level, their reign ceases, their influence is quenched, and their power disappears. Ah! sir, live—live in the bosom of the waters! There only is independence! There I recognise no masters! There I am free!

—Jules Verne, *20,000 Leagues Under the Sea* (1870)

Captain Nemo's submarine, *Nautilus,* is one of the most famous vessels to ever ply the seas of imagination or reality, and the captain and his ship have been inspiring prospective submariners for generations. Jules Verne's *20,000 Leagues Under the Sea,* first published in

25

1870, chronicles the adventures of Professor Aronnax, his butler Conseil, and a whaler named Ned Land. They are rescued from the ocean by the mysterious Captain Nemo and travel beneath the waves in his whalelike submarine, *Nautilus*. Nemo introduces his crew to dining on sea delicacies, smoking cigars made from tobacco-like sea plants, and walking on the floor of the ocean using scuba equipment. But the captain has a darker side: he likes to ram warships with his submarine, sinking them with all hands.

Verne's tale is remarkable for a number of reasons. He tells of a ship that can submerge beneath the waves, manufacture its own oxygen, and travel using electric power. Captain Nemo is self-sufficient, able to get everything he and his crew need to live from the ocean itself.

Verne's ideas were years before their time. Yet inventors had been experimenting with ideas of submarines since Leonardo da Vinci designed one while working for the Duke of Milan between 1485 and 1490. The first working submarine—powered, in fact, by electricity as the *Nautilus* was—would not appear until a few years after the publication of Verne's book. Scuba (*s*elf-*c*ontained *u*nderwater *b*reathing *a*pparatus) would not be invented until 1943. Verne, a Frenchman, would probably have been proud that the inventor of scuba was another Frenchman: Jacques Cousteau. Submarines would not be able to manufacture their own fresh oxygen until the world's first nuclear submarine—named *Nautilus* after Verne's creation—was launched in 1954. Nuclear power, an offshoot of the government project that invented the atomic bomb, allowed scientists to create a true submarine, a machine that could circle the globe underwater without ever needing to surface. A machine with only human limitations, the vessel would come home when the mission's three-month supply of food ran out.

Most historians attribute the first recorded submarine design to Leonardo da Vinci. However, da Vinci left out some crucial information: he never revealed how the sub was to be powered. Subsequent inventors attempted to build submarines, often with spectacular results. Historians credit Dr. Cornelius Van Drebble, a Dutch physician, with building and demonstrating the world's first functional submarine in 1620. Made of greased leather and wood, the underwater ship was powered by oars. Van Drebble presented his submarine in London, England, by submerging it in the Thames River, as King James I and crowds of British citizens looked on. When Van Drebble returned to the surface, he became a hero. Some historians doubt that the doctor created a true submarine, but at least the legend tells of his survival. Many other submarine inventors went down with their ships.

In 1774 John Day bought a wooden ship named *Maria* and created a watertight compartment on board. He planned to submerge the ship in the harbor at Plymouth, England, remain alive inside the watertight compartment for a time, and then drop his ballast stones and return to the surface. Day was so confident of his success that he took wagers on his chances, expecting to dive and then surface to cheers and a financial windfall. But the plan did not work out as he had envisioned. Day had no way of knowing that water pressure increases 15 pounds per square inch for every 30 feet of depth. At 130 feet the ship would have been subjected to 60 pounds of pressure per square inch. His ship reached the bottom, but Day drowned on the way down as the water pressure crushed the wooden vessel. John Day did indeed receive recognition, though not the type he sought: he has gone down in history as the first man to die aboard a submarine.

The American Revolutionary War saw the creation of a submarine by David Bushnell. Named *Turtle,* the small vessel carried one man, who was also its sole operator. The American navy designed the submarine to destroy enemy shipping by sneaking up to British vessels and screwing a timed explosive charge into the wooden keel. If the plan worked, once *Turtle* got far enough away, the device would go off and the British vessel would explode. *Turtle* never sank any ships, however, since the large explosive devices proved impossible to screw into the tough wooden planks of a ship's keel.

During the Civil War, submarine warfare took on a significant role. Historians credit CSS *Hunley,* a hand-powered Confederate navy submarine, with the first sinking of an enemy vessel by a sub. *Hunley* sank the Northern warship USS *Housatonic* on February 17, 1864, using a crude can torpedo. A can of gunpowder on a very long pole affixed to the front of the Confederate sub was rammed into the ship to set off the charge. However, the explosion that crippled *Housatonic* also appears to have opened the seams in *Hunley*'s cigar-shaped hull, allowing water to leak in. *Hunley* went down with all nine hands. In fact, the submarine had sunk many times before, causing the deaths of a total of 42 men, including its inventor. Interestingly, marine archeologists recently raised CSS *Hunley*, hoping to piece together what happened on its last and most intriguing mission.

Once a submarine sank a warship, the world of war was changed forever. Every nation with a navy began to worry about this undersea danger that could destroy prized battleships without warning. At the

time military leaders based their defense planning and strategies on the battleship, so the nation with the most battleships was considered the most powerful. Now navies had a new weapon; submarines allowed them to protect their own battleships and sink those of the enemy.

After determining that human-powered submarines and those made of wood were impractical, inventors began to work on new designs. Experimental vessels were powered by steam, electricity, diesel, gasoline, and chemicals such as hydrogen peroxide. Instead of wood, designers used riveted iron plate to streamline hulls.

With the help of modern technology, researchers raised and examined the Confederate submarine *Hunley* in April 2001. The vessel had been sunk during a battle in 1864, after successfully destroying the Northern warship USS *Housatonic*.

Many new submarine designs took to the water after the Civil War. Some designs were better than others, and inventors learned from their mistakes; but submarines are unforgiving, and the smallest miscalculations resulted in death. Submarines from 1865 to 1900 had colorful names: *Intelligent Whale, Nautilus, The Fenian Ram, Plunger, Argonaut, Narval, Peacemaker,* and *Porpoise.* They often suffered colorful fates, as well. Some exploded when toxic gases built up inside their hulls; others sank to the bottom and refused to come back to the surface; and some poisoned crews with chlorine gas from stubborn batteries or carbon monoxide from engine exhaust. Subs would sink with all hands, receive a refurbishing after being raised, and then sink all over again on the next voyage. It is no wonder the submarine service has traditionally been a volunteer service.

The Fenian Ram, Plunger, and *Porpoise* were all submarines built by an Irish-immigrant inventor named John Holland, a schoolteacher who lived in Paterson, New Jersey. His designs were some of the first reliable submarines, and he is considered the father of the U.S. submarine service.

Some jokingly refer to subs as "iron coffins"—a nickname a bystander invented after watching the *Holland II* founder on its test voyage. In 1900, the USS *Holland* (SS-1) became the U.S. Navy's first submarine purchase. Small by today's standards, the ship measured 53 feet long and carried a crew of seven. *Holland* featured equipment still used on submarines, including torpedoes and torpedo tubes, a periscope, and battery-powered electric motors for travel beneath the ocean's surface. John Holland's company, Electric Boat Company, still makes submarines for the navy at its shipyard in Groton, Connecticut, and some of his original submarines have been preserved and are on display in Paterson, New Jersey.

World War I saw extensive use of the submarine in combat. The Germans developed hundreds of subs referred to as U-boats—an abbreviation of *Untersee-boot,* which literally means underwater boat. U-boats first sank Allied merchant ships, destroying material needed in the British war effort. The U-boat then became a terror weapon when one sank the passenger liner *Lusitania* on May 7, 1915, killing 1,195 passengers. The action outraged the world and encouraged the United States—which up to that point had resisted participating in the war—to join the British and French in fighting the Germans. Although the British thought submarine warfare was an ungentlemanly way to fight, all nations noted the effectiveness of the sub as a weapon.

After the Germans lost World War I, they were prohibited from building submarines according to the terms of the Treaty of Versailles, signed in 1919. The Allies divided up the remaining German U-boats as spoils of war and then used the captured U-boat technology to improve their own subs. Unlike the Allied designs, U-boats were powered by diesel engines on the surface and battery-powered electric motors (which were charged by the diesels) underwater. The technology was especially valuable to the British, who at the time were using an extremely dangerous method—steam engines—to power some subs.

Ignoring the terms of the Treaty of Versailles, the Germans began building U-boats again during the 1930s as Hitler and the Nazi party militarized the Third Reich and once more positioned Germany for war. When World War II broke out, the Germans were again at an advantage over the Allies with their improved U-boats. These submarines could easily cross the Atlantic Ocean, and the Germans took the war literally to the shores of the United States.

U-boats controlled the Atlantic from the start of the war in 1939 until 1943. They sank more than 4,770 ships using wolf-pack techniques: groups of U-boats would attack single ships and convoys, much like a pack of wolves attacks prey. The U-boats would attack on the surface in daylight with impunity. Eventually, improved antisubmarine warfare and the overwhelming numbers of American ships and planes devoted to the U-boat problem turned the tide, and from mid-1943 until the war ended in 1945, the Germans lost U-boats in staggering numbers—a total of 740. For every 10 subs that left port, 7 or 8 never returned. German submariners refer to this period as "the sour pickle time."

The United States used its own fleet of submarines to great effect in the Pacific Ocean. These subs took the war to the shores of Japan, where, using wolf-pack techniques modeled after U-boat tactics, they sank thousands of tons of merchant and military shipping. During World War II the U.S. Navy lost 38 submarines to enemy action, with many of these losses occurring before they employed the wolf-pack techniques.

After Germany and Japan lost the war, the Allies again divided up the enemy submarines as part of the spoils. The subs were taken apart and analyzed, and their technology helped improve the next generation of vessels. Germany had been experimenting with snorkels for its submarines; the snorkel—which took up about the same amount of space as a trash can—allowed a diesel submarine to remain hidden below the surface, yet able to run its engines, charge the batteries, and freshen the air. This technology was

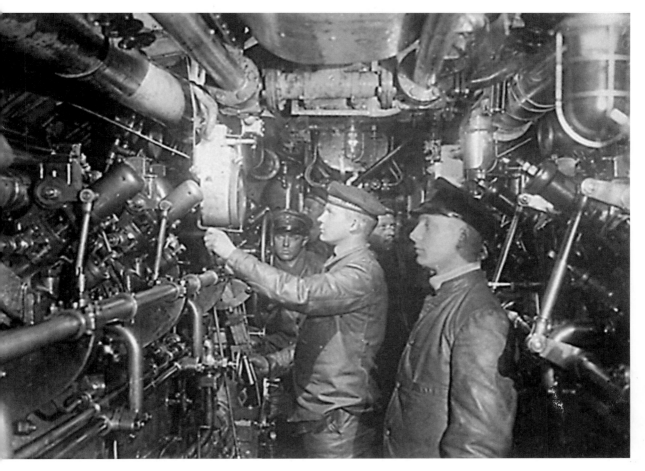

very valuable because it moved submariners closer to the ideal submarine, one that would never require surfacing. The less time a sub remains on the surface, the better. During wartime the reasons for remaining hidden are obvious—if a sub is spotted, it can be depth charged or torpedoed into oblivion. During peacetime, traveling along the surface of the ocean can be just as dangerous. Submarines are very hard to see in the open ocean, and many have been accidentally rammed by merchant ships.

A submarine with a snorkel is also very valuable for use in espionage. A spy sub can observe an enemy's

German sailors in the engine room of their World War I–era sub. Equipped with the latest submarine technology, German subs, or U-boats, presented a powerful threat to the United States and its allies.

German researchers pulled this U-boat, which had seen service during World War II, from the Baltic Sea in May 2001. After the war, the Allies had divided up surviving German submarines and copied the advanced design elements and technology.

shoreline or shipping activities or monitor radio transmissions without being detected. By the 1950s the United States and the USSR were no longer allies, and each side wanted to keep tabs on the other. The cold war helped spying become one of the primary missions of the attack-type submarine.

A U.S. Navy officer named Hyman Rickover saw another way besides the snorkel to design submarines. Making use of the technology of the mighty atomic bomb that ended World War II, he helped invent the first nuclear-powered submarine, *Nautilus,* which the

U.S. launched in 1954. In the process he became known as the father of the nuclear navy and was promoted to admiral. Admiral Rickover ruled over his nuclear submarines with a legendary iron fist until he was well into his eighties.

Since its invention, the submarine had always been a dirty place filled with unpleasant smells—diesel fumes, condensation, and the odor of rarely bathed crews. As a result, submarines were often referred to as "pigboats." But though the commander of a pigboat knew he would probably not rise any higher in rank, no proud submariner would switch from the "silent service," as submariners call their military duty, to the surface navy.

However, no one could call Rickover's atomic submarine a pigboat. *Nautilus* was clean, spacious, comfortable, and air-conditioned, and it did not smell of diesel fumes. The ship did not need to surface and could circle the globe without ever having to stop for fuel. The crew could even take occasional showers.

It is important to understand how a submarine works. A basic submarine is a tube of steel known as the pressure hull. Once the entrance hatches are closed to keep the water outside and the oxygen inside (for the crew), the tube descends in the water by using what are known as ballast tanks. Located outside the pressure hull, the ballast tanks are filled with water when the crew wishes to dive. The extra weight of the tanks makes the sub heavier than the surrounding water (known as negative buoyancy), and causes the ship to go down.

Wings on the outside of the sub, called diving planes, direct the sub's downward movement. Once the sub reaches the desired depth, the crew uses the planes and special smaller ballast tanks, called trim tanks, to keep the sub level and balanced. To make the sub surface, the crew purges the tanks of water and fills them with compressed air. The ship will rise because it has become lighter than the surrounding water (positive buoyancy). These basic principles govern the design of all submarines, regardless of what source is employed to power the ship.

On January 21, 1954, the first atomic-powered submarine, USS *Nautilus*, entered the Thames River at Groton, Connecticut, at its official launching. The event marked the beginning of a long race with the USSR to build the most powerful and energy-efficient nuclear vessel.

The USSR soon copied the design, and the nuclear submarine race followed the nuclear arms race.

The United States and the USSR experimented with designs of all kinds for their subs. Each came up with the Fleet Ballistic Missile submarine, or FBM. Slow, longer than a football field, completely silent, and capable of carrying and firing great numbers of nuclear-tipped ballistic missiles to targets anywhere on the globe, the FBM became an integral part of defense strategy. Today, the United States, Britain, France, and Russia all operate FBMs, which are shadowed by attack submarines designed to destroy them. The major military powers operate attack subs of various types, as well. These vessels operate year-round in the oceans of the world.

Still, as technologically advanced as submarines now are, as long as nations continue to build and operate these vessels there will be accidents. All submariners train against such an eventuality and rely on that training to help them to survive if and when an accident occurs. Nuclear submarine disasters add another level of difficulty to the problem: the nuclear fuels and weapons on board consist of some of the deadliest poisons known to man.

Thresher

The loss of the attack submarine USS *Thresher*, which sank off the coast of Massachusetts with 129 men aboard, shocked the American public and raised questions about the safety of nuclear warships.

3

The method of handling material in the United States [shipbuilding industry] was very, very sloppy.

—Frank T. Horan (engineer for *Nautilus*), quoted in *Forged in War*

On April 10, 1963, the nuclear-powered attack submarine USS *Thresher* (SSN-593) was conducting tests about 240 miles off the coast of Cape Cod, Massachusetts. *Thresher*, the first of a new class of deep-diving U.S. nuclear submarines, was capable of cruising at 1,000 feet below the surface and had a maximum depth (crush depth) of approximately 1,300 feet. *Thresher* was 279 feet long and 32 feet wide and usually carried a crew of 9 officers and 76 enlisted men.

It was the height of the cold war between the United States and the USSR. The two superpowers had gone to the brink of nuclear war during the Cuban missile crisis just a few short months before, in October 1962. The confrontation had ended when the Soviets had eventually removed their missiles from Cuba, but they were still building nuclear submarines to compete with the United States and NATO.

Soviet nuclear subs were rumored to be capable of traveling much deeper than American nuclear subs could. In response to this threat, the U.S. navy created *Thresher*. Its success would allow the navy to copy it and create a group of identical ships—Thresher-class submarines—that would be ready to fight the Soviets in deep waters. If the cold war turned hot, *Thresher*'s mission would be to hunt down and destroy Soviet fleet ballistic missile submarines (FBMs) before the Soviets could fire their nuclear missiles at the United States.

Thresher had just been repaired at Portsmouth Naval Shipyard in Kittery, Maine. When a ship has been repaired, or, in technical terms, has received a refitting or overhaul, it needs to go to sea for tests called sea trials—much like a mechanic's road test for a car after repairs. These trials ensure that every system on the ship has been fixed and is functioning correctly. During a refit, technicians also update ships with new equipment, and these new systems receive tests, as well.

Sea trials allow both new and old crew to become acquainted, or reacquainted, with the ship, learn to operate its new equipment, and make certain the vessel is ready to return to service. The biggest concern for a nuclear submarine (or any submarine for that matter) during these tests is the integrity of the hull.

Although some might joke that submarines are the only kind of ship designed to sink, these vessels can have absolutely no water leaks. On any ship a leak is hard to control, but since water pressure increases as a submarine travels deeper beneath the surface, at great depths a spray of pressurized water from a leak could be powerful enough to slice a man in half.

On the morning of April 10, *Thresher* was checking its hull for leaks as it tested its deep-diving capabilities. Its crew consisted of 129 men: 16 officers, 96 enlisted men, plus 17 civilian technicians (employees of the Portsmouth shipyard and representatives from the Naval Ordinance Laboratory). The sub was heading east along with USS *Skylark* (ASR-20), a submarine rescue ship, and the two vessels communicated via an underwater voice-powered telephone system. They traveled through the Georges Banks, a shallow commercial fishing area known for dangerous currents, then reached the area where the continental shelf dropped off, and the depth of the ocean changed from between 200 and 300 feet to more than 8,000 feet. This depth would allow *Thresher* enough room to perform some deep-diving tests.

At 7:50 A.M. *Thresher*'s lieutenant commander, Wes Harvey, gave the order to start the deep dive. Quartermaster Jackie Gunter informed *Skylark* that *Thresher* would be diving to 1,000 feet, and *Skylark* acknowledged the order. *Thresher*'s crew first took the submarine very slowly to 400 feet, while the crew and civilian technicians checked every surface of the hull and every hatch, seal, pipe, seam, and weld for leaks. They found none.

The hull of a nuclear submarine is basically a steel pipe with caps welded on the ends. Special steel is used in sub construction. For example, the commonly used

HY-80 steel can withstand pressures of up to 80,000 pounds per square inch—hence the 80 in its name. This single layer, just a few inches thick, is the only barrier against the crushing pressures of the ocean.

In a perfect submarine, the hull would consist of just one piece of impermeable steel, but in reality a nuclear submarine's hull is peppered with welds because it is constructed by fusing together a series of donut-shaped pieces of steel. Each "donut" is joined to the next, eventually creating the submarine's hydrodynamic, cigar-like shape. Inspectors x-ray each welded piece to certify its strength, and any piece that fails this rigorous test is torn apart and re-welded. Besides welds, a submarine's hull contains access hatches, periscopes, missile tubes, torpedo tubes, a propeller shaft, and numerous other openings necessary for the vessel to function—all of which must, of course, be watertight.

Thresher had been designed as an attack submarine. This kind of sub must be able to move quickly in order to surprise and destroy enemies. Because the thickness of the hull helps determine the weight and top speed of the submarine, attack submarines must be light. These vessels are like hot rods: they can "burn rubber" in case an enemy torpedo is heading its way. *Thresher*'s hull was just thick enough to withstand the pressures of deeper depths, but light enough so as not to sacrifice speed. But while U.S. nuclear submarines are fast because of their single hulls, this same design makes them more vulnerable to leakage. Soviet and Russian nuclear submarines use a double-hull design, increasing the odds the vessel could survive an accident or battle.

As testing procedures continued, *Thresher* maintained a depth of 400 feet for 50 minutes. At 9 A.M.

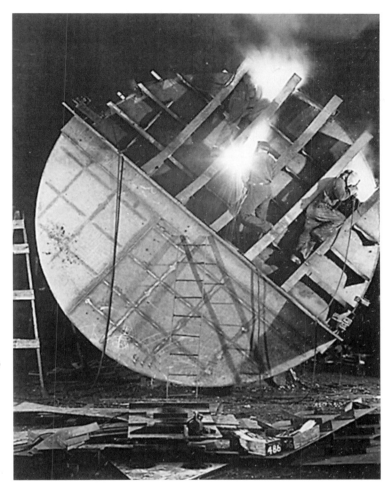

Workers at the Electric Boat Company in Groton, Connecticut, weld the donut-shaped pieces of steel used to construct the hull of a new submarine.

Lieutenant Commander Harvey ordered *Thresher* to descend to 1,000 feet. For every 33 feet of depth that a sub travels down, the water pressure on its hull increases by one atmosphere. At 1,000 feet, *Thresher* would be subjected to more than 30 atmospheres of pressure.

Quartermaster Gunter informed *Skylark* that *Thresher* would be proceeding deeper. The two men steering the ship pushed down on the airplane-like steering wheels that controlled the submarine, and the angle of *Thresher*'s dive increased. The submarine began to make creaks and groans as the outside water pressure increased. Though such noises are disconcerting, all submarines make them as they travel deep beneath the waves. It is a fact of physics that submarines cannot compress water; instead, water compresses a submarine. But engineers had designed *Thresher* to withstand the pressure, and the crew and civilian technicians continued to check everything to make certain the ship remained watertight.

At 9:12 things began to go wrong. At the test depth of 1,000 feet water began pouring into the ship. A pipe fitting had burst in the engine room, and seawater used for cooling the nuclear reactor was spraying everywhere. The men in the engine room contacted the control room and informed Lieutenant Commander Harvey of the problem. Harvey ordered the watertight doors between *Thresher*'s interior compartments closed. This contained the water to the engine room, where the men tried to staunch the flow of very cold, pressurized water.

The water sprayed onto vital electronic components, causing them to short out. Detecting the loss of power caused by the water damage, the safety sensors in the reactor automatically shut down the reactor— a procedural measure known as a reactor scram. Control rods made of graphite dropped into the reactor's uranium-235 core and stopped the reaction. With the reactor out of operation, no more steam was being produced and sent to the engine turbine. With the turbine stopped, the propeller did not turn.

Thresher was dead in the water.

The submarine was in a precarious position. It could not safely go much deeper than 1,000 feet, but as the ship filled with water, the extra weight was taking *Thresher* deeper. The reactor was off-line, and the sub badly needed that power because blowing the

ballast tanks would not provide a quick enough lift for a trip to the surface. *Thresher* needed to surface fast. Propeller power was required to drive the ship to the surface, but it would take seven minutes to restart the reactor and get the ship moving again.

Lieutenant Commander Harvey ordered an emergency blow of all ballast tanks, which usually means a last-resort dash to the surface. A submarine making an emergency blow will break the surface in a roar of air and water, sail into the air, and then fall back to the surface with a huge splash. But with *Thresher* the opposite happened. Because of the pressure at that depth, the lack of propulsion, the electrical problems, and the extra weight of the water, *Thresher* continued heading toward the bottom.

When its ballast tanks are blown, a submarine will quickly ascend to the ocean surface. This emergency blow procedure failed to save the stricken *Thresher*, however, and it continued its deadly descent to the bottom of the sea.

Skylark received a message at 9:13 A.M. from Lieutenant Commander Harvey: "Experiencing minor difficulty. Have positive up-angle. Attempting to blow." At 9:17 A.M. *Skylark* received another message: "Exceeding test depth." The men of *Skylark* then heard sickening sounds of crunching as *Thresher*'s hull imploded. At some point beyond *Thresher*'s crush depth, the ship was literally crushed and torn apart, killing all crew members and passengers within seconds. In his book *Explorations,* underwater explorer Robert D. Ballard imagines what happened:

> A crushing slab of seawater slammed into the ruptured pressure hull, tearing watertight bulkhead doors from their hinges like scraps of wet cardboard. The air inside the hull was instantly compressed to 750 pounds per square inch. *Thresher*'s hull became a huge combustion cylinder, the sea a piston. One hundred twenty-nine men were killed within seconds by the invisible blast of the superheated air. Diesel fuel and lubricants exploded. The thick curved flanks of the pressure hull were shredded. *Thresher* erupted like a giant depth charge.

The heavy pieces of the ship sank and came to rest at a depth of more than 8,000 feet below the ocean's surface. Oil, rubber gloves, pieces of cork, and other light materials from *Thresher* rose to the surface—but no bodies. *Skylark* stayed on location over the accident scene and relayed the news of *Thresher*'s disaster to shore.

The navy and the public were stunned that a nuclear submarine could be destroyed and disappear with all hands. *Nautilus*, the first nuclear submarine, had been an incredible achievement—a submarine that could travel underwater for years without need of surfacing, its only limits being those of its human crew. The American public was growing used to seeing pictures of U.S. nuclear submarines breaking through the ice of the North Pole. And American nuclear submarines patrolling the oceans were the first line of defense in the case of a nuclear attack from the USSR.

In the public's mind, U.S. scientists had beaten Japan with the atomic bomb, and now the atom had conquered the ocean. Soon U.S. scientists would put a man on the moon. Indeed, the invincibility of the U.S. military in general and its nuclear submarines in particular was so fixed in the American consciousness that Admiral Rickover and the navy were just as shocked and surprised as the public when *Thresher* did not return to port.

Rickover and his handpicked men had made sure that every possible safety precaution had been taken in the creation of the U.S. nuclear submarines. Rickover believed that *his* submarines, and he literally believed they were *his* personal property, had to be over-engineered for safety. In his view, the public would never allow the military a second chance if a meltdown or any other nuclear accident occurred on a submarine. He knew that any foul-up with the nuclear fuel that resulted in civilian contamination and casualties would spell the end for nuclear submarines.

Rickover and the navy went to work to find a cause for the disaster and ensure that a similar catastrophe would never occur again. It was not easy to get the desired answers. First, the navy needed to find the wreckage. There was a remote chance that *Thresher* had not been destroyed by accident. President John F. Kennedy needed to be sure that Soviets had not destroyed the sub or that *Thresher*'s crew had not

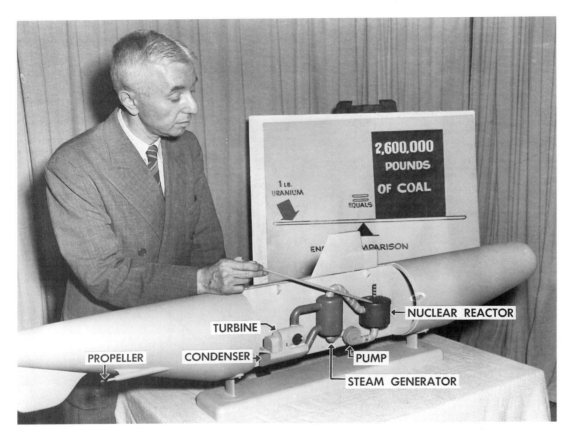

1 LB. URANIUM

EQUALS

2,600,000 POUNDS OF COAL

EN... ...MPARISON

NUCLEAR REACTOR

TURBINE

PROPELLER

CONDENSER

PUMP

STEAM GENERATOR

In this 1952 photograph, Captain Hyman Rickover, then director of the Nuclear Power Division of the Navy's Bureau of Ships, shows a model of the first atomic-powered submarine. Rickover believed that all necessary precautions had been taken to make nuclear submarines safe.

defected to the Soviet Union, taking the state-of-the-art submarine with them. The possibility also existed that radioactive material from the reactor vessel was leaking and poisoning the ocean. To put these fears to rest, the American people needed positive proof brought to the surface.

With *Thresher*'s wreckage lying at a depth of 8,000 feet, the navy had to use sonar to scan the seabed for images. Meanwhile, ships dragged long lines through the deep water, hoping to snag pieces of the sub. Sonar eventually found the approximate location of the wreck, and the search team brought a bathyscaphe (a small submersible designed for deep-sea exploration) called *Trieste* to the location.

Trieste looks like a submarine with a ball sticking out of its keel. Made of thick, high-strength steel, the ball has a window at which a crew of three sits. The rest of the craft is filled with high-octane aviation gasoline and magnetized iron pellets. *Trieste* descends and ascends by venting the gas and releasing these iron pellets. The bathyscaphe holds the record for the deepest dive ever—35,000 feet. However, compared with other subs *Trieste* has limited maneuvering capabilities: it functions solely as an elevator to the bottom, going down and coming back up.

In 1963 *Trieste* was one of the few submersibles capable of diving deep enough to look at the *Thresher's* wreckage. Using *Trieste,* scientists took many photographs of the wreckage of the sub. A piece of pipe and a few other items were recovered and brought to the surface. The pipe had serial numbers that conclusively linked it to *Thresher.* The condition of the wreckage was consistent with an accident. There were no telltale marks of a torpedo explosion or other type of attack. The navy also measured the level of radioactivity around the wreck and found no leakage of nuclear material. (In fact, to this day the navy continues to monitor *Thresher*, and to date there has been no release of nuclear materials.) This information helped put to rest the question of Soviet attack or possibility of defection of *Thresher's* crew.

Now the navy had two questions: What happened? And, would it happen again? After analyzing the recovered bits of *Thresher*; interpreting the wreckage photographs; conducting exhaustive tests; and interviewing scientists, engineers, sailors, and shipyard workers, the navy's investigators released their findings on the disaster. They believed the accident had been caused by the failure of a silver-brazed joint in a pipe in the reactor's seawater cooling system. Under the extreme pressures of the 1,000-foot depth, the pipe had exploded—and the water flowing from the pipe could not have entered the sub at a worse spot. The seawater had destroyed electrical circuits critical to reactor operations, causing the nuclear reactor to scram (run its emergency shutdown) and stop. Finally, after descending beyond its crush depth, the ship imploded. The navy's report was, of course, merely based on theory since *Thresher* was too deep to recover and there were no survivors to provide evidence.

Unless the government eventually recovers the wreckage, it cannot confirm the navy's theory, but with the discovery of many silver-brazed pipes from other nuclear submarines, the theory is beginning to gain more credence. A brazed joint is soldered together and is never as strong as a welded joint, in which metals are actually fused. The piece of pipe recovered from *Thresher* should have been welded to comply with U.S. Navy submarine specifications, and during *Thresher*'s construction, shipyard workers were supposed to weld everything. But in the claustrophobic interior of a submarine, some pipes were in locations nearly inaccessible to welders. Apparently, some workers had cut corners by brazing instead of welding, and inspectors had cut corners by not testing the pipes in those hard-to-reach locations.

The navy also found that *Thresher*'s ballast tanks had a serious design flaw. Though it is difficult, it is possible to blow ballast tanks despite the pressure of a deep dive. However, *Thresher*'s construction team had blundered by placing strainers in the piping systems that carried the air from the compressed air tanks to the ballast tanks. This design change was completed without consulting the navy, whose plan did not call for strainers in the pipes. When *Thresher*'s crew tried to pipe the compressed air to the ballast tanks to blow out the water and allow the ship to rise, ice had already formed on the strainers because of the change in pressure, a phenomenon called the Venturi effect. This same effect will cause an automobile carburetor to fill with ice on a cold day and stop the car's engine from running. Similarly, the ice clogged the pipes, preventing *Thresher*'s tanks from pumping out water. The navy subsequently found that other submarines had also been fitted with strainers and ordered them removed. In the construction of later submarines, larger pipes were installed to alleviate this problem.

This effort to increase the effectiveness of the emergency blow was part of the navy's SUBSAFE program, under the guidance of Dr. John P. Craven of the navy's Special Projects Office. Craven proposed a theory that the captain of *Thresher* might have spent precious moments checking the sonar to make sure the submarine would not hit a surface vessel when executing the emergency blow. Those extra seconds could have been enough to doom the vessel. Craven's theory motivated the navy to reevaluate the emergency blow procedures and come up with ways to speed up the process.

There are other theories about the loss of *Thresher,* as well. Some critics maintain that the navy's shock tests caused the disaster. In a shock test, explosives are dropped near a submarine to test its resistance to enemy depth charges. In 1963 this test was routine for all submarines. In the course of testing *Thresher*, some say, the explosions had been placed too close and damaged the pipe so it later burst during the deep dive.

Some analysts say that the HY-80 steel skin—at the time a brand-new steel, and *Thresher* was one of

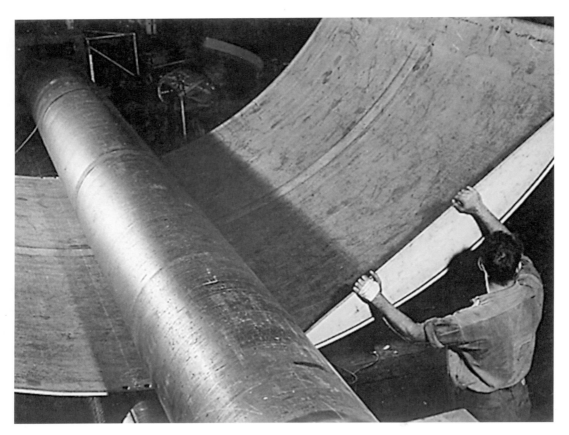

A submarine construction worker at the Electric Boat Company steadies a sheet of steel as it is shaped by giant rollers. Theories regarding the failure of the *Thresher* included the possibility that the sub's steel skin cracked because of a flaw introduced during its construction.

the first subs built with the material—cracked because of the shock testing. HY-80 is very brittle and fractures easily. If an impurity gets into a weld in HY-80, the steel will crack like an eggshell. During the construction of a submarine, each weld must be left alone for seven days to make sure it has not cracked. Perhaps the shock testing had proved too much for the brittle HY-80.

Others note that Admiral Rickover was an engineer by training, not a ship designer, and very good at designing conservative, robust nuclear reactors. Critics believe that in designing the nuclear submarine Rickover had focused on the reactor, and allowed critical flaws in other parts of the ship to escape his attention.

Another theory is primarily founded on the damage that *Thresher* sustained on previous voyages. Some believe a ballast tank damaged the year before might have been the cause of the accident. Still others believe the navy was using too many experimental materials in the submarine—such as flexible steam pipe couplings—that were not yet ready to go to sea.

Regardless of the cause, after the disaster the navy made certain that its stringent regulations were followed from the moment submarine construction began until the day the vessel was removed from service. In the construction of materials used for military purposes, rigorous specifications must be followed. Because military equipment must function in all types of weather conditions, as well as under enemy fire, construction standards must be high. If, for example, the sleeve of a winter army coat falls apart at the North Pole or a substandard pipe bursts on a navy submarine at 1,000 feet below the ocean, it becomes a matter of life and death. Still, accidents and mistakes happen with submarines because shipyard workers and navy crewmen are human and therefore fallible.

One example of human shortcomings occurred with *Nautilus*. The first nuclear submarine was almost destroyed because substandard piping was installed by mistake. Although its design standards called for seamless pipes made from a specific type of heavy-duty steel, shipyard workers took pipes from a dismantled grandstand—used, ironically, during a party for *Nautilus*. The substandard pipes had been stored next to the heavy-duty pipes meant for nuclear subs, and they ended up being inadvertently installed in *Nautilus* and other subs being built at the time. Later, during a dockside test of *Nautilus*'s reactor, the grandstand pipe exploded. Miraculously, no shipyard workers were seriously injured; but if the sub had been underwater, the accident might have destroyed the sub and its crew.

Because each piece of a nuclear submarine is marked with a serial number, and the pipe that exploded had no such number, investigators were able to figure out what happened after interviewing workers. The navy later instituted safeguards to ensure that substandard or counterfeit materials could not migrate into the system either at the subcontractor level or in the shipyard construction or refit process. The builder of *Nautilus,* the Electric Boat Company, made it a policy to use only seamless pipe in its shipyard to prevent another accident of this type from occurring again.

In addition to the construction safeguards, the navy addressed another element of safety. As part of the SUBSAFE program, Dr. John P. Craven was given charge of the creation of a Deep Submergence Rescue Vehicle (DSRV), a mini-submarine whose purpose was to rescue submariners trapped below the ocean's surface. At this time the navy had no modern program in place for saving its submariners. The navy did possess the McCann Rescue Chamber, a diving bell, but it counted on the sailors to save themselves by donning a Steinke-hood breathing device (which provides an air supply and serves as a flotation device) and swimming to the surface from a stricken submarine. This type of ascent is known as a free ascent.

It is unlikely that anyone will know for certain what happened to *Thresher,* but the 129 men on board did not die in vain. Because of their deaths, the navy created policies and equipment for the purpose of rescuing trapped submariners. It was also able to improve its subs and make them easier and safer to operate. And its newly instituted policies helped ensure that navy ships were constructed to conform to naval regulations.

The nuclear submarine program continued after the navy instituted its new policies. The Thresher-class subs became Permit-class subs, renamed after *Thresher*'s sister ship USS *Permit*. Before long, the U.S. Navy was prepared to do battle with the Soviets in the deep oceans.

The SUBSAFE Program

4

As of 1963 the U.S. Navy had no modern equipment for the rescue of trapped submariners—and there had been dozens of submarine disasters. The only rescue method in place depended on the sailors themselves. They were issued personal breathing devices and instructed in how to use them. If their submarine ran into trouble, they were expected to swim out of the sub and up to the surface for rescue—a very dangerous proposition under the best of circumstances.

There had been only one rescue of crewmen trapped underwater. That occurred in 1939 when the McCann Rescue Chamber saved 33 men from USS *Squalus*—the only time the chamber was used in a disaster. The McCann chamber had limitations: it was a diving bell, not a submarine; plus it required that cables be attached to the deck of the stricken submarine, so divers first had to get to the sub to attach the cables. Furthermore, the chamber could be attached only to a horizontal deck, and if the sub's deck was not reasonably level, the chamber would not work. Finally, if a lost sub was deeper than human divers could work, the guide cables could not be attached, and the submariners would die.

The U.S. Navy needed another way to save submarine crews.

Although many ideas had been presented as ways to save submariners, the navy preferred to develop submarines for combat use rather than for rescue purposes. Many still believed that Admiral Rickover's nuclear submarines were invincible—after all, they could supposedly run forever on their nuclear fuel. The only foreseeable loss of a submarine would be in combat against the Soviet Union, and in such a case there would probably be no survivors left to rescue. But accidents can influence change, and the *Thresher* disaster changed the navy's attitude.

After the *Thresher* disaster, the navy commissioned Dr. John P. Craven's Special Projects Office to create a submarine that could rescue the crews of sunken submarines. The resultant Deep Submergence Rescue Vehicle, created at great expense (the first model cost somewhere around $41 million), was cigar-shaped, 49 feet long and 8 feet wide, constructed of HY-140 steel, and propelled by a battery-powered electric motor. Under the HY-140 steel skin were three spheres: one for the operators, one for the airlock, and one for up to 24 survivors. The three-sphere design served a safety function. When a submarine is trapped on the bottom of the ocean, the air inside eventually becomes saturated with carbon dioxide from the air exhaled by survivors. Fouled air causes lethargy and affects the brain in odd ways—oxygen deprivation can cause a person to behave as if he or she were drunk. Therefore, the three-sphere design keeps a potentially dangerous rescued crewman from interfering with the operators of the DSRV.

In the event that the navy receives word of a nuclear submarine stranded beneath the surface, it will dispatch the DSRV. The mini-submarine travels attached to the deck of a mother sub to the disaster location. Once it arrives at the site, the DSRV crew opens the mother sub's exit hatch and climbs into the mini-sub. The DSRV lifts off and descends to the stricken sub. Upon reaching the stranded vessel, the crew of the rescue vehicle inspect the sub and then attach the DSRV to the best available escape hatch.

Unlike diving bells, which need a horizontal deck on which to attach and make an airtight seal, the DSRV has a docking mechanism and can adjust itself to a tilted deck of up to 45 degrees and make a proper seal, allowing survivors to climb into the DSRV and ride back to safety to the mother sub. A DSRV is capable of saving men trapped in American and NATO-type submarines and can descend to more than 3,000 feet below the surface (though its true maximum depth is kept secret).

Any sub that meets with disaster on the continental shelf of the coast of the United States can be assisted by a DSRV. The United States has two of them, *Mystic* and *Avalon*—one for each coast—and they are ready to be airlifted by cargo jet to any submarine disaster at any time, in any location in the world. But so far the navy has never used a DSRV in an actual emergency.

An interesting aside to the story of the DSRV is its use as an undersea spy vehicle. The DSRV program ran many millions of dollars over budget, prompting a Senate investigation—in fact, Wisconsin senator William Proxmire "honored" the DSRV with his Golden Fleece

(continued on page 62)

"SUBMARINE DOWN OFF NEW ENGLAND COAST"

In 1939 the U.S. Navy made headlines around the world when 33 men aboard the USS *Squalus* (SS-192) were rescued. *Squalus* was a new fleet-type submarine, 310 feet long and 28 feet wide. On May 23, the submarine left Portsmouth Naval Shipyard for sea trials. Lieutenant Oliver Naquin was in charge. Aboard were 59 men: 5 officers, 51 enlisted men, and 3 civilian observers from the shipyard.

Naquin was putting the ship through diving tests that day to ensure that *Squalus* was ready for service. At 8:40 A.M. *Squalus* dived and was unable to come back to the surface. The sub came to rest on the bottom, 240 feet below the surface. A main induction valve for the diesel engines had failed to close, and half the ship flooded. Twenty-six men drowned in the accident, while 33 men in the front half of the ship waited on the bottom for help.

"Submarine Down Off New England Coast" read the newspaper headline on

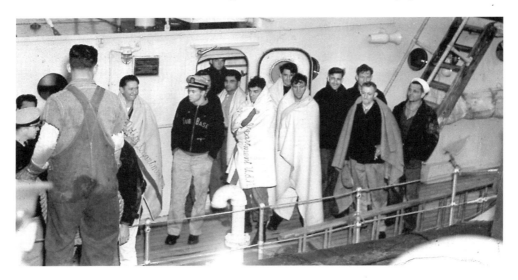

Survivors of the USS Squalus, *which sank on May 23, 1939, stand on the open deck of a U.S. Coast Guard ship as it carries them to Portsmouth, New Hampshire. A newly developed diving bell, called the McCann Rescue Chamber, brought the men to safety a day after the sinking.*

May 24, 1939. The entire world waited for word on the missing submarine. The U.S. Navy acted quickly and dispatched diving expert Lieutenant Commander Swede Momsen to the scene. A submariner himself, Momsen had been working for years on methods for rescuing trapped submariners. Before 1939 no navy with submarines in service had come up with a way of saving men trapped at the bottom of the sea. The U.S. Navy did not like to be reminded of that fact, and Momsen's career had suffered because of it. But Momsen had continued his work and helped design an experimental device called the McCann Rescue Chamber.

Momsen and his divers arrived at the scene aboard USS *Falcon*. Ship divers quickly descended to *Squalus* and attached guidelines on either side of the sub's forward escape hatch. The McCann Rescue Chamber, which resembled an upside-down coffee can, traveled down these lines to the deck and was attached over the hatch. All told, the diving chamber made five trips to the sub and brought back all 33 survivors.

The device worked perfectly except for the last trip to the surface, when the cable connected to it began to unravel, and the chamber could not move. It was a dicey moment. If the cable snapped, the chamber would tumble to the bottom of the sea, and all the men inside would drown. Momsen made a split-second decision to haul the chamber up by hand. The crew of *Falcon* worked as a team, carefully pulling the chamber to the surface. Oliver Naquin, the submarine's skipper, was the last man out. The U.S. Navy had successfully rescued the first submariners trapped on the bottom of the ocean, and Swede Momsen became a hero.

The rescue had not been an easy one by any measure. The depth of 240 feet was beyond the limits of safe diving, and the divers involved in setting the guidelines for the rescue chamber risked suffering from the bends. Any sudden change in pressure from a slip and fall from the deck of *Squalus* as they attached the lines would have instantly killed a diver with the "squeeze"—the diver's body would have been instantly compressed into his helmet.

The rescue led by Momsen seemed even more impressive after Britain's *Thetis* disaster in July 1939. That sub's front torpedo room flooded, and *Thetis* was stuck with its bow on the bottom and its stern just below the surface. Four men made it out, but 99 died. Without a device like the McCann Rescue Chamber, no one on the surface could help them.

The Deep Submergence Rescue Vehicle *Mystic* (DSRV1) is moved from the naval air station at North Island, California, for air-lift transport to Turkey, where it would be used in NATO submarine rescue exercises in the Mediterranean Sea.

(continued from page 59)

award because, he said, the program wasted so many tax dollars. It was revealed in two books, *Blind Man's Bluff* and *The Silent War*, that the DSRV program ran over budget because the Special Projects Office used it to spy on the USSR. This particular use of the DSRV was top secret, and the Senate's grumbling over the wasted tax dollars was an effective smokescreen for the Special Projects Office.

Craven and others realized the DSRV would probably

never be needed because most submarines travel in waters too deep for DSRV-assisted rescues. The laws of physics state that no one would survive aboard a submarine headed to the bottom of the deep ocean. Still, the DSRV would be a perfect vessel for spy missions. It could tap underwater telephone lines and gather sunken enemy equipment—all far from the sight of enemies. It is quite possible, even though the cold war has ended, that the navy is still using the DSRV for classified spy missions.

Scorpion

It took several months to locate the USS *Scorpion*, seen here at its July 1960 launching ceremony, after it disappeared on May 27, 1968. Even after the sub was found, researchers could not definitely say what had caused the loss of the nuclear submarine.

5

If something can be installed backward, it will be.

—John P. Craven

On the afternoon of May 27, 1968, the families and friends of the crew of USS *Scorpion* (SSN-589) were gathered on a dock at the Norfolk, Virginia, naval base. The submarine had been gone since February 15, 1968, and those who were gathered could hardly wait to see their husbands, fathers, brothers, and boyfriends. The men of the *Scorpion* had been at sea for three months and had a lot of catching up to do with friends and loved ones. *Scorpion* was due to arrive at 12:40 P.M., and the people gathered at the dock waited in a light rain, watching the water, hoping to catch the first glimpse of the rounded hydrodynamic hull of the fast-attack submarine.

The scheduled arrival time came and went with no sign of *Scorpion*, but most members of the waiting group didn't worry. They figured that the submarine was just running late. After all, *Scorpion*'s activities were top secret and a matter of national security. Perhaps the submarine had completed a mission that took longer than expected. This was a way of life for nuclear submarine families: the missions were secret and so they never knew where the submariners were for months at a time.

However, as the minutes turned to hours, the people gathered began to suspect something had happened to *Scorpion*. The navy began to wonder, as well. The last message from the submarine had been received on May 21. Lieutenant Commander Francis A. Slattery had given his position as 50 miles south of the Azores Islands, near Portugal, and indicated that the sub was on its way home. The crew had been silent ever since; *Scorpion* had sent no message that morning to inform Norfolk of its position and projected arrival time. At 3:15 P.M. on May 27, 1968, the navy informed the world that USS *Scorpion* was missing. The families and friends of *Scorpion*'s crew left the dock in stunned silence, praying the navy's message was a mistake. But it was no mistake. *Scorpion* was gone, along with 99 crewmen. The U.S. Navy had lost its second nuclear submarine within a five-year period.

In May 1968 the United States was embroiled in the Vietnam War, and antiwar sentiment gripped the nation. At the same time the U.S. Navy's nuclear submarine force was hard at work shadowing the Soviet nuclear submarine force, protecting against possible nuclear attack. *Scorpion* had been cruising the Mediterranean Sea, observing Soviet activities and taking part in antisubmarine training exercises with foreign navies.

Scorpion was a Skipjack-class nuclear fast-attack submarine. Launched in 1958 and commissioned in 1960, it was 252 feet long and 32 feet wide, capable of traveling at more than 20 knots per hour in the water. On this mission the sub had been armed with the Mark 37 torpedo. *Scorpion* also carried a reliable crew. Lieutenant Commander Francis A. Slattery and his 99 fellow shipmates had received commendations for their leadership and professionalism on earlier missions.

The captain and his crew had made this trip to the Mediterranean before, and *Scorpion* had received an overhaul just a year earlier, so it seemed unlikely that a mechanical failure had occurred. The navy had made many changes after the loss of *Thresher,* but had the military overlooked another problem in the American nuclear submarine program? Had *Scorpion* hit an uncharted underwater object and disappeared? Had *Scorpion* collided with a Soviet submarine? Other American submarines had hit underwater objects and suffered significant damage. And collisions between Soviet and U.S. Navy submarines had occurred before, as the two sides observed each other's operations. In fact, in December 1967, just six months earlier, USS *George C. Marshall,* a fleet ballistic-missile submarine, had collided with a Soviet attack submarine in the Mediterranean.

President Lyndon B. Johnson had only one question: Had *Scorpion* been sunk by the Soviets? If so, it was an act of war. The U.S. Navy needed to find *Scorpion* fast in order to answer all these questions, but the problem of locating it seemed immense: the submarine could be anywhere beneath the 3,000 miles of ocean between Spain and Norfolk, Virginia.

The navy began the search by sending ships to *Scorpion*'s last known location, and it brought in Dr. John P. Craven of the Special Projects Office to lead the investigation. In 1966 Craven had found a lost U.S. Air Force hydrogen bomb in the Mediterranean by using Bayes' theorem of subjective probability. Thomas Bayes was an 18th-century mathematician who constructed a formula used to make a series of educated guesses concerning the whereabouts of a missing item. In usual practice, his obscure theorem is a way to place a bet where the missing item in question is the jackpot.

Craven was an enthusiastic poker player, so the gambling cachet of the theory appealed to him as a means to locate *Scorpion*: Bets are assigned levels of probable reliability whereby a grid is constructed; this grid then becomes the map for a search area. Although Bayes' theorem might at first glance generate a search grid that appears counterintuitive to an experienced search professional, Craven's offbeat mathematical approach had in fact helped the air force retrieve a nuclear weapon from the Mediterranean on April 7, 1966, after weeks of fruitless searching.

Craven realized there were probably sound recordings of *Scorpion*'s last moments. The U.S. Navy and the U.S. Air Force both had hydrophones (underwater microphones) positioned at strategic locations in the oceans; the navy's network of hydrophones (abbreviated as SOSUS for *so*und *su*rveillance *s*ystem) was used to eavesdrop on the underwater activities of Soviet submarines.

SOSUS technicians listening to the hydrophones collected recordings of the passing Soviet submarines. Because each sub has a distinctive sound pattern, or signature, the U.S. Navy could track and record the

entire missions of individual Soviet submarines. The skilled technicians could note a submarine's speed, course, and noise emissions from internal machinery, and even speculate on a vessel's condition and repair status. SOSUS, combined with satellite photographs of Soviet naval bases, spies on the ground in Soviet naval bases, U.S. Navy patrol planes, and navy submarines shadowing Soviet submarines, gave the U.S. military intelligence a comprehensive understanding of Soviet submarine activities.

Checking SOSUS seemed like a good idea, but it turned out that the network had picked up nothing because the equipment was calibrated to pick up noises

An oceanographic cable ship. To search for sunken ships, the vessel trails a cable that carries camera equipment or sonar sensors behind it. Navy investigators eventually photographed *Scorpion*'s wreckage using equipment towed by USNS *Mizar*.

from submarines, like propeller noise, and filter out pops, explosions, and other similar sounds that occur for a number of reasons in oceans. Craven then asked a colleague named Gordon Hamilton, who ran an oceanographic laboratory in Bermuda, if he had any hydrophones positioned in the Atlantic. It turned out he had one in the water at a lab in the Canary Islands— very close, in fact, to *Scorpion*'s last known position. The records from the lab were collected. They revealed that loud noises had been generated in the area between May 21 and May 27.

Craven's team found other records from air force hydrophones located in Newfoundland. When put together, the records allowed Craven to determine that two enormous explosions, just 91 seconds apart, had occurred along *Scorpion*'s expected course. This information indicated that *Scorpion* was most definitely lost with all hands. The water in this area was miles deep, and two underwater explosions that were large enough to register on equipment as far away as Newfoundland would certainly have destroyed the submarine before the men had a chance to escape.

Other intelligence information indicated that there had been no Soviet activity in the area during the time of *Scorpion*'s passage. Officials informed President Johnson that the Soviets had nothing to do with the submarine's loss. One part of the *Scorpion* mystery, at least, was answered.

USNS *Mizar* was sent to the coordinates that Craven determined as the site of the explosions. While *Mizar* and other ships were hunting for *Scorpion,* Craven kept working and calculating. He noticed that *Scorpion* appeared to be heading back toward Europe, not toward the United States, and he also discovered the reason: a runaway torpedo. A submarine will turn

180 degrees during an emergency maneuver to stop a runaway torpedo, known to submariners as a "hot run." The guidance system of a torpedo contains safety mechanisms that will deactivate if the vessel turns around, preventing it from destroying the very sub that launched it. (This is an unlikely occurrence, but it has happened: USS *Tang,* one of the most successful submarines of World War II, was sunk by its own torpedo during a battle on October 24, 1944; 73 men died, and 15 of its survivors were imprisoned by the Japanese navy.) Submarine commanders drill until this maneuver becomes second nature. *Scorpion* had plenty of destructive force on board; aside from the 14 Mark 37 torpedoes, it was also armed with 7 Mark 14 torpedoes and 2 nuclear-tipped Astor torpedoes.

In December 1967 a hot run had taken place on *Scorpion*, and Lieutenant Commander Slattery had acted quickly and saved the sub. Craven found out that other hot runs had happened on submarines. The navy had sent out a bulletin warning that it was possible to install electric leads on test equipment in reverse order, and that later this faulty equipment could activate a torpedo during servicing. (Sailors service their equipment often, and this work goes on whether the ship is on a cruise or tied up at a dock.)

Craven theorized that one of the torpedoes had been tested with incorrectly installed equipment, which started a hot run, and though Slattery managed to turn the ship, he had not been fast enough. The torpedo's explosion would have killed the men in the torpedo room, possibly detonating other torpedoes in the process The breached hull would have sent *Scorpion* toward the bottom until it passed its crush depth and imploded.

However, the navy did not take Craven's theory of

Dr. John P. Craven led the navy investigation that determined *Scorpion*'s most likely resting place. He later theorized that the sub had been destroyed by one of its own torpedoes.

a runaway torpedo seriously. The Ordinance Systems Command stated that a hot run was impossible, but it did not provide any evidence to back up this claim. Undeterred, Craven continued to work, while Chester "Buck" Buchanan, a civilian oceanographer and Naval Research Laboratory scientist, continued to search for *Scorpion* using cameras towed by *Mizar*.

Craven used Bayes' theorem to construct a map of the wreck site. His crew made bets on the torpedo theory, *Scorpion*'s course heading during what they believed was a hot run, and the landing spot of the wreckage on the bottom. Meanwhile, the navy found some wreckage—a pipe and other items—and became convinced the investigators were on the right track.

The months of June, July, and August passed without finding *Scorpion*. Finally Buchanan began searching the coordinates provided by Craven. On October 29, 1968, the nuclear submarine was found more than 11,000 feet underwater in the Atlantic Ocean, 200 miles southwest from the Azores, on the edge of the Sargasso Sea—just 220 yards from where Craven and his team predicted it would be (although its exact location remains classified). Craven had done it again.

Mizar's cameras took many photos of the wreckage, and the navy sent the bathyscaphe *Trieste II* down to examine the wreck. Observers found *Scorpion* largely intact but crushed from the extreme water pressure. There appeared to have been no survivors, and no bodies were ever found. Nor was there evidence of a hole from a torpedo explosion. However, the hatches in the bow of the ship were missing, which could have been caused by an explosion inside the torpedo room.

In January 1969 the navy released a press release that read, in part, that there was "no incontrovertible proof of the exact cause" of the submarine's destruction. In 1993, after the end of the cold war, the navy released its full report from 1969. Its number one supposition was that a hot-running torpedo sank *Scorpion*.

It is unfortunate that the cause of *Scorpion*'s sinking may never be known, but there are numerous theories about what happened to the submarine. *Scorpion* had not yet been outfitted with the new SUBSAFE changes, so it is possible that a mechanical failure sent the submarine to the bottom. Perhaps the sub was destroyed because it did not have the improved emergency blow capabilities and other SUBSAFE improvements.

Some analysts theorize that a massive explosion in *Scorpion*'s battery compartment caused the sub's destruction. Because storage batteries generate hydrogen gas when they are charging, a nearby spark could cause an explosion. Battery explosions have been the cause of many sub disasters, so this theory is plausible. The wreckage of many subs shows damage to their battery compartments for precisely this reason.

Perhaps the most intriguing theory concerns something John Craven found out many years later. A defect existed in some of the batteries that powered the Mark 37 torpedo; some of them had a tendency to explode during random durability tests. The batteries that exploded were manufactured by a company that had never made batteries before—and their recall had been ordered at about the same time that *Scorpion* was destroyed.

The batteries had been manufactured with cheap, fragile foil diaphragms. Unfortunately the cheap foil could be partially punctured by the sloshing of a battery's electrolyte, which may have been caused by the vibrations occurring during the submarine's normal operations. Powering up the battery prematurely would heat the battery's three-foot-long body, and since the battery was located next to the 330-pound, highly explosive warhead of the torpedo, the great heat generated by the cooking battery could have been enough to ignite the explosive.

Experts theorize that a defective, overheated battery caused the torpedo to either completely explode or partially "cook off"—a slow burning or partial detonation of the warhead. Either instance would have been enough to blow a hatch or crack the hull, causing water to instantly flood the torpedo

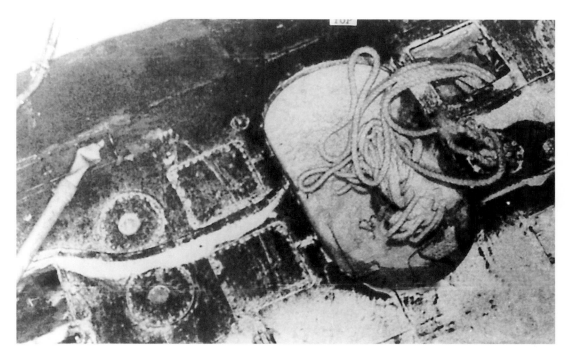

room and sink the *Scorpion*. A piece of foil that cost pennies possibly caused the loss of the sub and the deaths of its crew. Making matters even worse, the navy had known about the bad batteries, but because it needed submarines to shadow Soviet operations so badly, it approved their use anyway.

The U.S. Navy checks the wreckage site of *Scorpion* periodically for radiation leakage, and so far none has been detected. The wrecks of warships are owned forever by their countries of origin, unlike civilian vessels like *Titanic,* which are governed by the laws of salvage. The U.S. Navy's official word on *Scorpion* is that the wreckage site is classified, and the cause of the accident is unknown. Pictures taken by the divers aboard the *Trieste II* in 1968 and by explorer Robert Ballard in 1986 have been released to the public. For years *Scorpion*'s mysterious accident has haunted the navy and the families of the disaster victims.

This 1968 photograph shows the top of *Scorpion*, which remains more than 11,000 underwater in the Atlantic Ocean. The center right circle, which contains a mooring line, is a cavity normally used for storing a messenger buoy. Also visible are circular main ballast tank vents and two rectangular hatches of the sub.

Russian
Disasters

A Soviet nuclear submarine, damaged on the hull near its conning tower, sits motionless in the waters of the Atlantic. The USSR produced a great number of these vessels, often with little regard to safety. As a result, most nuclear submarine accidents have involved ships belonging to the Soviets.

6

It had happened before to other men in other Soviet boats; one crew rode out a terrible gale, trapped in the after compartment of a burned-out hulk of a sub that refused to sink. They'd sealed themselves up and lived for three weeks until the submarine was towed into port. No light, no food other than what they'd stuffed into their pockets, no water except what they could drain from lines passing through the space. It was unimaginable.

—A description of the 1972 K-19 accident from *Hostile Waters*

During the cold war, the Soviet Union constructed and operated more submarines than the United States, the United Kingdom, and France combined. The USSR launched its first nuclear submarine K-3 in 1957, just two years after *Nautilus,* the world's first nuclear submarine, slid down the ways. After that vessel's creation, the Soviets experimented with nuclear subs of various types. They built vessels with twin propellers and twin nuclear reactors; they constructed submarines with titanium hulls that were capable of diving far deeper than American submarines; they created subs that were faster than American submarines and employed ingenious propulsion designs that made them extremely quiet; and they constructed many types of nuclear reactors, some of which used liquid metal as coolant.

The U.S. Navy's nuclear submarine program was conservative in approach both because of Admiral Rickover's emphasis on safety and because the program was beholden to the American taxpayer. In contrast, the Soviet's communist regime never solicited the opinions of the citizens, and the government invested heavily in its submarine program, siphoning money from social programs to fund it. In the book *Running Critical,* Patrick Tyler notes that the Soviets outspent the United States 10 to 1 in the early 1970s. Because of its lack of budgetary concerns, the Soviet navy could afford to experiment with designs, materials, and reactors. Its nuclear submarine program was secret, as well. If a submarine did not perform to expectations, the Soviet navy never reported it to the public.

The USSR also attempted to keep its submarine disasters secret, but too many accidents occurred for this policy to work. The environmental group Greenpeace estimates that 121 Soviet nuclear submarine accidents took place over the years. The Russian newspaper *Izvestia* estimates 507 men have died since the Russian nuclear submarine program began. It is impossible to fix an exact number of accidents because of the Soviet-era policy of secrecy, but during the 1990s the Russians released information when it declassified files from this time. Many accidents occurred because the Soviet navy put a very low priority on crew safety and other important matters. It built submarines without many of the safety systems found on American and NATO submarines; both the crews and the environment suffered as a result.

Some Soviet submarines were light and fast underwater, able to keep pace with an aircraft carrier traveling 18 to 20 knots. But they were fast because they were built without using the proper amount of lead shielding—a very heavy metal—for the nuclear reactors. This shielding prevents radiation produced by the reactor from escaping the chamber and harming the crew. American designers, on the other hand, were not allowed to use lighter materials and so built U.S. nuclear submarines with the proper shielding. Therefore, since the designers had the Los Angeles-class attack subs built for speed to combat the faster Soviet subs, as a compromise they made the hull thinner to cut weight. Consequently, Los Angeles-class submarines were fast and able to keep pace with their Soviet counterparts, but they were not able to dive deep.

On July 4, 1961, the Soviets suffered their first nuclear submarine accident. K-19, a Hotel-class ballistic-missile submarine, developed a leak in its reactor cooling system, resulting in irradiation of the entire interior of the submarine. Although the crew was evacuated, and K-19 was towed into port, nine men died from radiation poisoning and burns received when they shut down the nuclear reactor. According to an August 2000 *New York Times* article, the sailors referred to their work in the reactor chamber as stepping "into the Boa's Mouth." K-19 earned the dubious nickname "Hiroshima," after the site of the U.S. atom bomb attack on Japan at the close of World War II.

It is hard to speculate what the U.S. Navy would have done in case like the K-19 incident, but it most likely would have scrapped an irradiated submarine. The Soviets, however, simply removed the damaged reactor equipment from K-19, installed new reactor equipment, refitted the sub, and sent it on patrol with a new crew.

Less than a year later, in June 1962, the November-class submarine K-3, the Soviet Union's first nuclear submarine, suffered a severe reactor fire. The public does not yet know if any casualties resulted from this accident, but it is reasonable to suspect that there were. The submarine was overhauled for two years and then returned to service. As part of the overhaul, the damaged reactor was cut out of the vessel and disposed of—dumped into the Kara Sea. The ill-fated K-3 was then plagued by yet another accident. On September 8, 1967, a fire broke out in the ship's hydraulic system, and 39 men died.

In 1968 at least two more Soviet submarines suffered disasters. On April 11, 1968, the Golf-class submarine K-129, a diesel-powered ballistic-missile submarine, sank in the Pacific Ocean. K-129 was carrying a full complement of nuclear-tipped missiles when an explosion of unknown origin sent it more than 16,000 feet to the bottom with all hands. Although the Soviets searched frantically for the sub, they couldn't locate the wreckage.

K-129 was an obsolete diesel submarine equipped with obsolete missiles, and would not bear mention except for the fact that the CIA spent hundreds of millions of dollars in a failed secret attempt to pluck the sunken sub from the ocean. Again using Bayes' theorem, John Craven of the Special Projects Office had pinpointed K-129's exact location. The navy then secretly photographed the wreckage, which showed that the submarine was not crushed, but had landed intact on the bottom. The most likely explanation for this is that the sub filled immediately and completely with water after a sudden

The November-class K-3 sub was the Soviet Union's first nuclear-powered submarine. It would suffer from two major accidents during its service in the Soviet navy.

explosion, and because the pressures both inside and outside the hull were equalized, water pressure did not flatten the vessel.

The CIA eventually took control of K-129's wreck site in a mission called Project Jennifer. Craven and the navy watched from the sidelines as the CIA created an elaborate cover story for the media, involving millionaire

Howard Hughes, the mining of manganese nodules from the bottom of the ocean, and a huge ship named *Glomar Explorer*. This ship carried deep-sea drilling equipment, which the CIA modified for use as a deep-sea crane. The recovery vessel lowered the crane's grapple to the wreck and clamped onto the submarine. It took many hours for the crane to slowly raise the waterlogged submarine from the bottom, and then somewhere along the way the grapple failed. K-129 broke apart and fell back to the seabed. The part of the sub that landed shattered on impact, though a small portion of the sub was retrieved. The human remains found inside were buried with full military honors; the burial service was videotaped, and the tape was presented to the Russians after the end of the cold war. Nothing of value was retrieved from K-129.

The second reported Soviet submarine disaster of 1968 happened on May 24. K-27, a November-class nuclear submarine, was at sea when an undetermined reactor accident occurred, and nine men died from radiation poisoning. Also in 1968, according to some reports, an unidentified nuclear submarine went down in the Arctic Ocean. This report cannot be substantiated, but if the report is true there is a submarine containing the remains of 90 men and a reactor filled with radioactive fuel on the sea bottom off the Kola Peninsula.

The Soviet navy's bad luck continued. On April 8, 1970, November-class submarine K-8 had a major fire. The K-8's crew got off the sub, which was dead in the water, and the submarine was taken under tow. Moscow then ordered the men to return to the stricken sub to make sure it did not sink during the tow. About half the crew returned to the sub. The captain and 51 crewmen drowned when the vessel suddenly sank in the Bay of Biscay on April 12, 1970.

On February 24, 1972, K-19—the same vessel that had been nicknamed Hiroshima after its 1961 radiation leak in the reactor cooling system—had a major fire, and 28 crewmen were killed. Twelve men who had remained on board in an attempt to extinguish the flames eventually became trapped in the rear compartments of the submarine. K-19 was taken under tow, but the trapped men could not be released from the submarine while it was on the open ocean. The crewmen rode in the darkness and stale air of the stricken submarine for 24 days until shipyard workers with torches cut a hole in the hull and released them.

Another major reactor accident occurred on June 13, 1973, on the nuclear-powered Echo II–class cruise-missile submarine K-56. Twenty-seven men died. Then on September 26, 1976, eight men died in a fire on Echo II–class K-46.

The 1980s saw a continuation of Soviet nuclear-submarine disasters. On August 21, 1980, nine men were killed in a fire on another Echo II-class submarine. And in August 1982 Alpha-class submarine K-123 developed a coolant leak in its liquid metal-cooled nuclear reactor. No casualties were reported, but the sub was out of commission for eight years; the duration of the overhaul suggests how severe the accident was. On June 24, 1983, a Charlie class–cruise-missile submarine, K-429, sank in the North Pacific Ocean. Most of the crew on board died, but the Soviets eventually salvaged the vessel—one of the few occasions when nuclear materials have been removed from a submarine wreck site.

Disaster was narrowly averted on October 6, 1986, when a Yankee-class–ballistic-missile submarine, K-219, sank near Bermuda after a missile explosion. Ballistic-missile submarines are affectionately nicknamed boomers because of the explosive payloads of their

U.S. Navy surveillance aircraft photographed this Soviet Yankee-class nuclear-powered submarine, the K-219, as it foundered off the coast of Bermuda in October 1986.

missiles—and K-219 carried 15 missiles, each armed with two 600-kiloton thermonuclear warheads. The missiles contained a liquid fuel composed of nitrogen tetroxide and hydrazine.

When seawater leaked into one of the missile tubes through a faulty gasket, it mixed with the nitrogen tetroxide and formed nitric acid. This nitric acid burned through the missile's casing and caused the hydrazine and the nitrogen tetroxide to combine. When these chemicals ordinarily mix to provide thrust for the missile, it is supposed to happen in a controlled fashion; in this case, the mixing caused an explosion. The blast blew the hatch from the top of the missile's tube, and water flooded into the submarine. Fires broke out, and the submarine almost went to the bottom. Remarkably, Captain Igor Britanov was able to bring K-219 back to the surface, and the crew battled to save the submarine.

On that day, USS *Augusta* (SSN-710), a Los Angeles–class attack submarine, was shadowing the Soviet sub. U.S. subs shadowed Soviet boomers from the moment they left port until the moment they returned. *Augusta*'s crew observed the incident and at first thought K-219 was preparing to launch a missile targeting the United States. Crew members went so far as to prepare torpedoes for firing before they realized that the Soviet submarine was in trouble. *Augusta* remained on location for the entire accident, silently observing, recording, and reporting everything.

K-219's fires began to heat the missiles in their tubes, creating the danger of another explosion—possibly a nuclear one. The fires had burned through the wires connected to the reactor's remote control panels, making it impossible for the men in the sub's control room, forward of the damaged and burning missile room, to control K-219's twin nuclear reactors. If the reactors had melted down while the submarine was on the surface, the cloud of nuclear fallout would have enveloped the East Coast of the United States.

The reactors were out of control, and the only way to turn them off was to crank the control baffles into place by hand. This emergency maneuver required a man to climb inside each reactor to turn the crank—a heroic feat that would result in sterilization and leukemia for the crewman if he was lucky, and a painful, gruesome death from acute radiation poisoning if he was not. In addition to the crises of the fires and the out-of-control reactors, the nitric acid from the missiles was eating through the rubber gaskets of the ship. Noxious fumes seeped through the hatches that the crew had sealed to protect themselves, and the men were running out of replacement canisters of oxygen for their emergency breathing devices. If the sub became uninhabitable, they would have to abandon ship.

Two crewmen saved the day. Engineer-Seaman Sergei Preminin and Senior Lieutenant Nikolai Belikov hand cranked the reactor control baffles into place and prevented a catastrophic meltdown. In the atmosphere of the reactor space, Preminin succumbed to the poisonous fumes, unable to escape because of the heat and the pressure difference, which had sealed the exit hatch and prevented it from being opened. He was posthumously awarded the Red Star for bravery. Belikov did not receive a Red Star; he did receive a greater award, he survived the ordeal.

Despite the bravery of the two crewmen, K-219 could not be saved, and the men abandoned ship. To prevent the sub's capture by the U.S. Navy ships that had gathered to observe the disaster, Captain Britanov scuttled the sub, sinking it in 18,000 feet of water. A total of four men died in the accident. A book—written by Peter Hutchthausen, Igor Kurdin, and R. Alan White—and a television movie, both titled *Hostile Waters,* tell the story of this event. Many articles and news stories have described the accident—but to this day the U.S. Navy refuses to comment on the K-219 incident.

It is interesting to note that K-219 might never have suffered an accident except for the Soviet reluctance to create safer solid-fuel rockets for submarines. The U.S. Navy had been using solid-fuel missiles for its boomers from the first Polaris-fleet–ballistic-missile submarines in the early 1960s. The solid fuel was so safe that it was shaped into objects like ashtrays to prove the point.

The Soviet Union suffered two more accidents that decade, both in 1989. On April 7, 1989, the Mike-class–nuclear-powered submarine K-278 sank, killing

most of the crew, after a fire in the Norwegian Sea on its maiden voyage. Some reports indicate there was only one survivor. This man and five other crewmen climbed into the escape pod, located in the sail of the submarine. Unfortunately they did not know how to operate the pod properly, and only one survived the trip to the surface.

K-278, named *Komsomolets,* was capable of diving deeper than any American or NATO submarine because its hull was constructed entirely of titanium. Titanium is one of the strongest, rarest, and most expensive metals on the planet—though it is difficult to work with since it cannot be welded in a room with oxygen; welders must

Rutger Hauer appears as Captain Igor Britanov in a scene from the 1997 television movie *Hostile Waters.* The film was based on the near disaster involving the Soviet sub K-219, which caught fire and came close to setting off a nuclear explosion that would have affected the East Coast of the United States.

dress in space suits to perform hull welds in an atmosphere of argon gas—and the Soviet Union had great reserves of it. Ironically, in 1989, parts of the Soviet Union were without basic human amenities like food and sanitation, yet the government was capable of building titanium-hulled submarines.

There was talk of raising *Komsomolets* because of its nuclear fuel, but the project never began. Reportedly, the Soviets encased the sub in a gel or glue that sealed it from the corrosion of the sea.

The final accident of the decade involving a Soviet nuclear submarine occurred in June 1989, when Echo II–class submarine K-192 had a major reactor incident. It is unknown if any casualties resulted, but the submarine was removed from service, which suggests that a severe accident took place. Navies usually remove a sub from service when it has been exposed to extreme radiation contamination.

From 1990 until the *Kursk* accident of 2000, the pace of accidents slowed—partly because the fall of communism and the end of the Soviet Union left the Russian navy with a shortage of money to operate many submarines. But though the accident rate slowed, the accidents didn't stop.

In 1991 a Typhoon-class boomer had a mishap with a missile during a training exercise. The Russians refer to this sub as *Akula,* and it is gigantic: 561 feet long, 79 feet wide, and capable of carrying 20 ballistic missiles. Then on January 26, 1998, the last major accident before the *Kursk* disaster occurred when an Oscar II–class submarine named *Tomsk* had an explosion in its reactor cooling system. One crewman died, and five others were hospitalized.

Perhaps the biggest accident is yet to come. The Russian navy still sends submarines to sea, though it operates on a shoestring budget. The government generates some capital by selling its small diesel-electric Kilo-class submarines to any nation in the world with hard currency. The money helps, but most of the once-vast Russian Northern Fleet is tied up at dockside, awaiting overhaul or decommissioning. The submarines —some reportedly barely afloat—are still loaded with radioactive fuel, though their radioactivity is not closely monitored. As a result they pose a hazard both to the Russian people and the entire world. It remains to be seen what will become of these vessels. Russia lacks the funds necessary to dispose of them, and the United States has not attempted to help. The possibility looms that the nuclear material in these submarines could poison the ocean or be vented into the atmosphere if an explosion, fire, or meltdown were to occur.

A lack of Russian interest in submarine safety concerns continues to place not only its own naval personnel, but also the entire world, in jeopardy.

Kursk

A rescue diving bell. In the days following the sinking of *Kursk,* the Russians tried unsuccessfully to lower a diving bell from the rescue ship *Altay* to the hatch of the stricken sub. They eventually had to give up because of rough seas and the bitterly cold arctic weather.

After Oscar-II-class submarine K-149, named *Kursk,* sank in the Barents Sea on August 12, 2000, the Russian navy attempted to rescue the 118 men trapped on board. Navy spokesmen were optimistic at first, predicting that the men would be rescued quickly. They reported receiving radio messages from the crew, plus vigorously tapped coded messages. They also reported receiving a message stating that all the sailors were alive and well.

The Russian navy brought a diving bell, referred to as a Bester, to the wreck site and lowered it 350 feet from the churning surface of the Barents Sea to *Kursk* many times—but with no success in sealing it to one of the submarine's escape hatches. The rescuers could not secure guidelines to the deck of *Kursk,* and the bell dangled at the end of its tether. The men guiding the bell kept hoping it would latch onto the right spot, but their task was equivalent to using a magnet on a string to pick up a nail while standing atop a 35-story building.

Further complicating their task were two factors: bad weather on the surface and the fact that *Kursk* was resting at a 60-degree angle. In 1939 Swede Momsen and the survivors of *Squalus* had been lucky because their stricken sub rested perfectly level on the bottom. The men of *Kursk* were not as fortunate. It was very difficult, if not impossible, for the diving bell to make a proper seal at that angle.

The Russian navy also possessed a rescue submarine, but it was reportedly either laid up for repairs at the time of the accident or out of commission because of a lack of repair funds. Other Russian mini-subs were sent to the area, but they were not capable of docking with the stricken *Kursk*. The U.S. Navy offered its DSRV to help in the rescue, but the Russians refused American help. (In point of fact, though, while the DSRV can seal to the hatches of American and NATO ships, it probably would not have been able to seal to the hatches of *Kursk*.)

The Russians eventually asked for help from the Norwegian and British navies. The British government dispatched its rescue submarine *LR-5,* which arrived on the scene on Saturday, August 19, seven days after *Kursk* sank. But too much time had passed; the oxygen supply for the men had run out. The tapping hammer had gone silent. The 118 men on board the submarine were dead. Norwegian divers were able to get down to the sub and open the rear escape hatch, something the Russians had not been able to do. They found the sub completely filled with water.

The Russians had wasted a lot of time during the *Kursk* disaster. They also further complicated the situation

with misinformation and interference. According to one of the Norwegian divers, Øystein Olav Noss, quoted on *CNN.com,* the Russians restricted the movements of the Norwegian divers working on *Kursk*. "They drew a circle on the middle section of the sub. Anything outside a radius of 25 meters from the hatch was off limits," Noss said. The Russians refused American help throughout the disaster, possibly because they did not want the U.S. Navy to see secret submarine technology or weapons. Russian statements that there had been radio contact with survivors and that the sub had oxygen supplies that would last at least two weeks were later retracted. There might have been vigorous tapping from the *Kursk* survivors at first, but after further analysis, many naval experts and

Norwegian divers Rune Spjelkavik (left) and Paal Stefan Dinessen make preparations for their dive to the *Kursk* on Sunday, August 20, 2000. Because the escape hatch of the submarine was badly damaged, a British mini-sub could not attach to the sub, so Russian officials turned to the divers for help.

scientists believed that any taps from survivors were short-lived. In addition, the double-hull design of the sub would have made it very hard for a tap to be heard outside, so most likely the taps came from trapped air escaping from chambers within the hull.

Divers entered the submarine through hatches and holes cut into the hull with plasma torches. The work was extremely dangerous. At 350 feet below the surface, the divers were at the limits of safe diving and had to use special gas mixtures and decompression chambers to combat the effects of oxygen narcosis and the bends. Divers could have been killed by the extreme pressure and cold if their protective suits had been punctured by jagged pieces of debris.

Indeed, Russian admiral Vladimir Kuroyedov reminded the divers of the dangers, telling them that their lives were more important than the retrieval of bodies or artifacts. "You should think of your families," he said. "We understand you are capable of anything, but remember that your lives are more important to me today."

Exercising extreme caution, the divers managed to recover 12 bodies, two messages, and the ship's log from the rear compartments of the sub before they suspended their work because of winter weather. The chambers they examined showed evidence of fire. The logbook had no entry concerning the accident. The two messages, found with the bodies of sailors, shed light on the last hours on the ship. An unknown sailor wrote, "There are 23 people in the ninth compartment. We feel bad . . . we're weakened by the effects of carbon monoxide from the fire . . . the pressure is increasing in the compartment. . . . If we head for the surface we won't survive the compression."

Lieutenant-Captain Dmitry Kolesnikov, 23 years old, wrote, "All personnel from sections six, seven and eight

The first body recovered from *Kursk* was identified as that of Lieutenant-Captain Dmitry Kolesnikov. In this August 1998 photograph he proudly posed on the submarine that would cause his death.

have moved to section nine [the last compartment of the stern]. There are 23 people here. We have made the decision because none of us can escape." Kolesnikov also mentioned that the men were not able to open the escape hatch, which they referred to as the escape trunk. This chamber has one hatch on the top and one on the bottom. To escape, a sailor opens the bottom hatch, climbs inside, and closes the hatch behind him. He then dons his emergency breathing hood and floods the chamber with water. Flooding equalizes the pressure between the escape trunk and the water above the top hatch. Without equalizing the pressure, the hatch cannot be opened due to the level of water pressure bearing down on it. When the pressures are equal, the top hatch bursts open, and the sailor inside can make a free ascent to the surface.

It is possible that something may have happened to the hatch on *Kursk*. Perhaps the explosion or the jolt as the ship struck bottom jammed the hatch. A lack of training could also have prevented the men from attempting an escape. It was reported that the men of *Komsomolets* had had no idea how to work their escape equipment, and had read the instruction manual for the escape pod just before they attempted to use it. Perhaps a similar lack of training prevented the crewmen of *Kursk* from opening the hatch.

On the surface, a number of factors helped to doom *Kursk*. The Russian navy was slow to notice it had lost a sub. Ineptitude, a lack of equipment, a lack of trained men to operate the equipment, obstinacy, a fear of the West, bad weather, and bad luck all worked against the men trapped on the bottom of Barents Sea. The cause of the accident was alternately chalked up to friendly fire, a collision with an unknown U.S. submarine, a World War II mine, malfunction of a torpedo, espionage, human error, and sabotage.

The most probable explanation for the accident was a torpedo explosion in either the torpedo room or the torpedo tube. The divers found that the submarine showed massive damage consistent with a torpedo explosion in the bow, where the torpedo room is located. *Kursk* was test-firing torpedoes during its training exercises, and the men in the torpedo room were preparing torpedoes for launch. Perhaps there was a hot run and the torpedo exploded before it could be deactivated, or the torpedo exploded before the crewmen even loaded it. In either scenario the accidental explosion would have been an utter catastrophe, detonating the other torpedoes in the compartment and killing everyone in the room. The explosion registered as strong as a small earthquake on nearby seismographs, so it is likely that most of the weapons in the torpedo room did detonate. This explosion sent *Kursk* to the bottom.

The Russians have stated that *Kursk* was carrying new torpedoes propelled by liquid fuel instead of solid fuel or compressed air. Experts point out that the Russians have a history of accidents with liquid fuel and submarines. (K-219 went to the bottom when a liquid-fueled ballistic missile exploded inside the submarine.) If the fuel had exploded, it would have created a huge fireball and shockwave capable of blowing through the submarine at the speed of sound, killing or seriously injuring much of the crew before anyone knew what had happened.

It is also possible that friendly fire from the vessels participating in the training exercise may have sunk *Kursk*. In a training exercise, anything can happen, so a torpedo, mine, or depth charge used in the exercise could have sunk *Kursk* by accident. The Russian navy had not conducted training exercises on such a large scale for many years. Many untrained or partially trained men were taking part, which could have increased the chance of an accident. However, both the Russians and Americans have stated that friendly fire did not destroy the sub.

Indeed, the Russians maintain that an American or British submarine observing the exercises got too close and collided with *Kursk*, and the force of this collision crippled and sank the submarine. However, while many collisions occurred between American and Soviet submarines during the cold war, and some of the subs were damaged beyond repair, there is no record of a nuclear submarine being destroyed by a collision with another nuclear submarine. Furthermore, the Americans and British both emphatically deny that their submarines collided with *Kursk* or any other Russian vessel during the exercise. Two U.S. Navy submarines, USS *Memphis* (SSN-691) and USS *Toledo* (SSN-769), were in the area monitoring the exercises. They are not known to have suffered any damage.

The *Kursk* disaster fascinated and infuriated the world. Reports of the accident and the trapped crewmen filled newspapers, magazines, TV programs, and the Internet. The story became even more fascinating when the Norwegian divers finally opened the sub's escape hatch. If the Russians had swallowed their pride and asked for help faster, there may have been survivors from the accident.

This information, along with pictures taken at the time of Russian president Vladimir Putin enjoying his summer vacation—instead of cutting it short to deal with the emergency—enraged the families of the *Kursk* sailors and many Russian people. Putin eventually apologized and expressed his sadness. "I have a great feeling of responsibility and guilt for this tragedy," he said on August 23, 2000, but his approval rating still suffered because of his lack of attention to the incident. Rumors spread throughout the country that the navy did not want to save the submariners because they would reveal to the world the true condition of the Russian navy.

The disaster infuriated environmentalists around the world because it involved yet another Russian nuclear submarine. The Russians have the dubious distinction of having deposited the most nuclear submarine material on the ocean floor. Organizations like Bellona are monitoring *Kursk* along with the other Russian submarines and reactors resting on the bottom of the world's oceans.

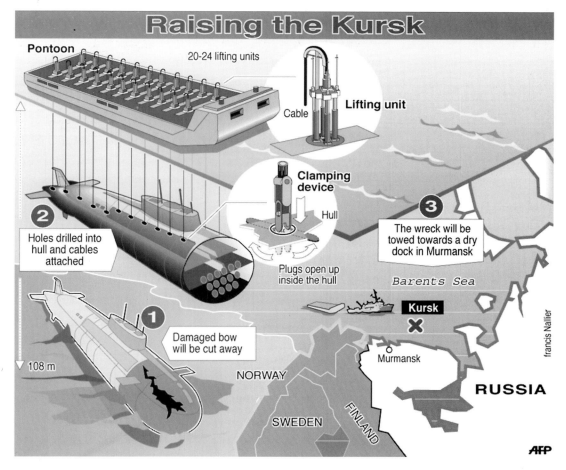

Raising the Kursk

Pontoon

20-24 lifting units

Cable

Lifting unit

Clamping device

Hull

Plugs open up inside the hull

2 Holes drilled into hull and cables attached

1 Damaged bow will be cut away

▽ 108 m

3 The wreck will be towed towards a dry dock in Murmansk

Barents Sea

Kursk ✕

Murmansk

NORWAY

SWEDEN

FINLAND

RUSSIA

francis Nallier

AFP

The most fascinating aspect to the *Kursk* story is the attempt to raise the vessel. According to news reports published in May 2001, the Dutch salvage firm Mammoet planned to raise the submarine by September 10, 2001, and by the summer of 2001 workers had already begun to prepare the site. From practically the day the submarine sank, there had been talk of raising it. An international effort led by the *Kursk* Foundation, located in Brussels, Belgium, began raising money for the operation as soon as the submarine went down—it was estimated that approximately $70 to $80 million was required for the job.

Successfully raising the submarine would prevent the

An illustration published in June 2001 outlines the risks involved with raising the *Kursk* submarine from its watery tomb 350 feet below the surface of the Barents Sea.

nuclear fuel contained in its two reactors from contaminating the Barents Sea and nearby fishing grounds. It would also allow the Russians to determine exactly what caused the accident and prevent a similar incident from occurring again. There may be an unknown defect in the Oscar II–class submarines still in service, and being able to examine the wreckage would help scientists learn if there is a class-specific problem. An inspection of the *Kursk* wreckage would also help scientists figure out if there was a problem or defect that could affect the entire Russian submarine fleet. The information contained in the wreckage might also inspire the Russian navy to finally create a program like the U.S. SUBSAFE program.

Submarines have been raised from the ocean before. In 1939 Swede Momsen not only saved the men of *Squalus,* he also raised the sub and hauled it back to the Portsmouth navy yard for overhaul. This part of the job was more dangerous than saving the men, requiring many dives to prepare the sub. The divers risked the bends and the squeeze among other hazards, and there were mishaps. Luckily, no lives were lost in the salvage operation.

The divers used technology similar to what would be needed to raise *Kursk*. Air-filled pontoons raised *Squalus* to just below the water's surface, and ships then towed it into Portsmouth. *Kursk* would probably require the same type of recovery. For an effective salvage, divers need to descend to the wreck and clear channels underneath the sub. The salvage team has to pass cables under the sub through these chambers, which are secured to balloons inflated with nitrogen. Next, the team drills holes into the hull, making the cables fast to the hull. The inflated balloons would then lift the submarine off the seabed. Finally, the vessel can then be secured to a tow ship and hauled back to port.

Another method of recovery would entail cutting holes in the hull and securing cables that would be attached to giant cranes on the surface. In that case, *Kursk* would be pulled up by the cranes, secured, and towed back to port. Once *Kursk* reaches port it presumably will be dry-docked for removal of the reactors and bodies, then inspected to determine a cause of the tragedy.

The Russians have indicated that they will cut the damaged bow section from the sub before lifting it from the bottom. They say they will retrieve this portion later and without foreign help. This may mean a secret weapon of some sort is inside the bow. Whatever the reason, this would make raising the sub much safer because there would be no danger of torpedo explosion.

The raising of a nuclear submarine will be dangerous enough as it is. There is a risk of meltdown or explosion if the ship tilts as it is being raised. The control rods could come out of the reactors, causing a nuclear reaction to begin again. It is hard to predict what could result from tilting twin nuclear reactors sideways or upside down—it is quite possible that some type of devastating explosion might occur.

The Russians hope to be able to raise *Kursk* without incident, recover the lost bodies of the crew, and determine what happened. The grieving families of the 118 men who died deserve an answer.

An Accident Can Be the Impetus for Reform

In the United States, the SUBSAFE program has helped ensure that better, safer designs and materials are used for submarines under construction. Existing subs have also been retrofitted according to the safety commission's specifications.

Many nuclear submarine disasters have occurred since the world's first nuclear submarine, *Nautilus*, was launched in 1954. Two U.S. Navy submarines (*Thresher* and *Scorpion*) and at least four Soviet/Russian navy submarines (K-8, K-219, *Komsomolets,* and *Kursk*) rest on the bottom of the world's oceans. Because nuclear materials are deadly poisons and take many years to decay into nontoxic materials, the wrecks of nuclear subs and their discarded reactors and fuel will have to be boldly marked on ocean maps and monitored for thousands of years to come. These sites are toxic dumps and must not be disturbed.

Critics note that an accident is often the only impetus for reform. This is very true with nuclear submarine disasters. With the successful launching of *Nautilus*, the United States went on a public-relations blitz promoting "good old American know-how." The entire nation was temporarily lulled into a false sense of security. *Nautilus* had problems, but the government never revealed them to the public. It could not, however, cover up the loss of *Thresher* with all its hands. The disaster brought the U.S. Navy and the nation back to reality.

The navy instituted the SUBSAFE program in 1963 as a result of the *Thresher* disaster. All nuclear submarines under construction were given better ballast systems built to strict navy specifications, while submarines already built and in service were retrofitted with SUBSAFE equipment during overhaul. Ballast pipes were enlarged for better operation, and dangerous strainers that could cause ice formation and blockage were removed from the pipes.

After the loss of *Thresher,* officials cracked down on contractors and workers, demanding stringent adherence to navy specifications. From the first to the last day of a nuclear submarine's construction, workers and contractors had to stick to these specifications at all times. Only equipment, spare parts, and raw materials that had been approved would make it into U.S. Navy nuclear submarines. Such restrictions would prevent a reactor pipe explosion like the one that happened on board *Nautilus* from ever occurring again.

SUBSAFE also demanded that each weld specified in a submarine's design would actually be welded, and checked. The safety commission would not allow for the brazing of pipes wherever a weld was specified. Another reform from SUBSAFE called for redundancy in the construction of electrical systems. Redundancy in this case simply means doubling up on equipment—two systems that do the same job, so if one breaks down, the other can take over. The electrical equipment that failed on *Thresher* might have continued operating if there

had been better redundancy in the system. Yet another SUBSAFE reform called for the curtailment of experimental equipment in active-duty submarines. *Thresher* had some experimental flexible steam-pipe couplings, and while they are not believed to have contributed to the accident, SUBSAFE believed that experiments with equipment should be performed in test subs, not active-duty ones.

SUBSAFE also evaluated the emergency blow procedure, which the safety commission streamlined for maximum efficiency. The new system allowed for faster implementation of the emergency blow, in the hopes of saving a submarine and preventing disaster. On February 9, 2001, while entertaining a group of

National Transportation Safety Board members inspect the USS *Greeneville* (SSN-772) as it sits in dry dock at the Pearl Harbor Naval Shipyard. In February 2001, while demonstrating an emergency blow procedure off the coast of Hawaii, the *Greeneville* struck a Japanese fishing vessel, sinking the ship and killing nine people.

political campaign donors aboard a thank-you cruise, the Los Angeles–class attack submarine USS *Greeneville* (SSN-772) performed an exhibition emergency blow, during which it collided with a Japanese high school–training ship, *Ehime Maru*. In this case, crew personnel did not properly follow the safety procedures, and four students and five sailors were killed when the sub shot up to the surface. At this writing no known changes have been made to the emergency blow procedure following this submarine disaster.

The biggest ramification of SUBSAFE was the development in the 1960s of the Deep Submergence Rescue Vehicle, a tiny submarine capable of diving down to a stricken sub and rescuing the crew members trapped inside. It travels to a wreck site on the back of a nuclear submarine and performs all of its functions underwater. Before the creation of the DSRV, the U.S. Navy had only the McCann Rescue Chamber and individual deep-sea diving equipment to perform rescue operations. With the development of this mini-sub, it became possible to save any submarine crews trapped on the bottom of shallow waters.

When the DSRV was created, nothing like it had existed before. The head of SUBSAFE, John P. Craven, and others had noted the difficulties in operating equipment in the depths of the ocean. The extreme water pressure and cold, plus the lack of breathable oxygen, create problems for underwater rescue efforts similar to the difficulties faced by astronauts exploring the vacuum of outer space. A piece of equipment built for the ocean must endure its brutal habitat; the ocean will find any flaw in a craft and destroy it.

Aside from its value as a rescue vessel, the DSRV has also helped to advance the science of underwater exploration. Technological advances have been made because of programs that created the DSRV and other rescue craft like the British *LR-5*. Some of these innovations helped scientists find *Titanic* and will be used in the future to find other wrecks of value to military personnel and historians alike.

While the DSRV has never been used in a disaster, it has been used as a spy vehicle. Because it is able to arrive at a location, perform its mission, and leave without ever breaking the surface, it is ideal for such purposes. The DSRV's spy missions are classified, but many believe that during the cold war the vessel was used to tap underwater Soviet phone lines and retrieve pieces of sunken classified military equipment from the Soviets' ocean test sites. Perhaps information regarding the DSRV's classified missions will be released in the future through requests under the Freedom of Information Act.

It is not known if the Russians have a program like SUBSAFE to avert future disasters. If they have had one, it can be inferred that it must not have worked very well because over the years the Soviet and Russian governments have lost four complete submarines and suffered dozens of other accidents. The crews suffered, as well, with an estimated 507 men killed or injured in nuclear submarine accidents.

Whether or not the Russians have a program like SUBSAFE, they do have two excellent submarine safety ideas. The double-hull submarine designs have helped the Russian vessels that meet with disaster through acts of war or accidents remain in one piece. If a sub ends up on the sea bottom, the robust double-hull design may also help contain nuclear materials in the vessel.

Russian submarine designers have also included in their subs escape pods that are large enough to save an entire crew. An escape pod is a clever idea—though in actuality a pod has only been used in an emergency once, when in 1989 a sailor escaped in one from *Komsomolets* as it sank on its maiden voyage. The United States and NATO submarines have nothing like escape pods installed in their submarines, and they would do well to try to include such devices in future vessels—especially if the subs dive deeper than existing rescue submarines can reach.

The Russians have also experimented with rescue submarines and mini-subs, but as of the turn of the 21st century, they do not have the financial resources to properly maintain and operate the equipment. In fact, they barely have the finances to operate their once-great navy or train their sailors. The Russians must reevaluate their place in the world and figure out how large a navy they actually need and can afford. Some analysts speculate that Russia will soon only operate a coastal naval fleet for self-protection.

The Russians may stop using liquid-fueled weaponry on their submarines, as well. As was evident from the liquid-fueled missile explosion that destroyed K-219—and, most likely, the *Kursk*—an accident with liquid-fuel inside a sealed submarine can be catastrophic. Solid fuel is much more stable, and the U.S. Navy has used it in submarine missiles since the Polaris submarine ballistic-missile program of the early 1960s.

The entire world was watching as the drama of the *Kursk* disaster unfolded. Perhaps the international interest in the fate of the sub and in its raising will benefit the Russian people as well. They need billions of dollars and the services of brilliant scientists and skilled workers to clean up all of their dangerous leftover cold war–era nuclear submarines and nuclear materials. If the raising of *Kursk* doesn't draw attention to this dangerous problem, then perhaps forward-thinking politicians, scientists, and environmentalists will influence world opinion to find a

As more nations have added submarines to their navy programs, more subs cruise the waters of the world than ever before. The proliferation of nuclear submarines has greatly enhanced the odds that deadly accidents will continue to occur.

solution to eliminating the nuclear dangers lurking in Russian harbors and shipyards.

It is also important to note that the world proliferation of submarines is still ongoing. Russia, Germany, and Sweden produce new, sophisticated diesel-electric submarines for sale to any nation with the money to purchase one, and the United States and Britain sometimes sell or give their decommissioned diesel-electric subs to friendly nations. Taiwan is planning to purchase new diesel-electric submarines from Germany with the help of the United States. China will probably purchase or build more subs to combat international threats to its security. Pakistan is supposedly creating a diesel-powered fleet ballistic-missile submarine for use in its fledgling nuclear-arms race with India. There has been no word from India on its submarine wish list, but presumably Indian scientists and marine engineers are working on a design to match Pakistan's. Only time will tell.

One thing is certain: The history of the submarine is intertwined with the stories of subs that have met with disasters, accidents, and death. Submariners refer to those unfortunate vessels and crews lost in the ocean depths as being on "eternal patrol." Nuclear submarines will continue to operate in the 21st century with enhanced stealth technologies and more advanced weaponry. The United States, Britain, France, and Russia will continue to use nuclear submarines because they are integral to their country's naval defense strategies. And more accidents will occur, but perhaps these accidents will not be serious disasters for the crews or for the environment.

The Russians have suffered the most accidents and casualties, having constructed and operated more submarines than the United States and NATO combined during the cold war, and with little regard for crew safety. Their policy of dumping nuclear materials into the ocean instead of placing them in lead or cement containment vaults has shown little regard for the environment, as well. Such a course of action may eventually poison ocean fishing grounds, make certain areas of the world uninhabitable, and pose other problems such as increased cancer and infant mortality rates, as well as decreased life span and quality of life in certain parts of the earth.

Many concerned citizens hope that Russia will team up with the United States and NATO countries and discontinue such environmentally disastrous policies. Perhaps, too, with improvements in rescue equipment and training, fewer nuclear-submarine disasters will occur in the 21st century.

Chronology

1620	Doctor Cornelius Van Drebble, a Dutch physician, builds and demonstrates the world's first functional submarine
1774	John Day dies while demonstrating his submarine *Maria*, a converted wooden sloop, at Plymouth, England; becomes the first person to die in a submarine accident
1776	During the Revolutionary War, the American navy uses *Turtle*, a small submarine powered by one man, in an attempt to destroy British vessels
1864	On February 17, CSS *Hunley*, a hand-powered Confederate navy submarine, sinks the USS *Housatonic,* the first warship destroyed by a submarine in combat
1900	USS *Holland* (SS-1) becomes the first submarine purchased by the U.S. Navy; it features torpedoes and torpedo tubes, a periscope, and battery-powered electric motors, as well as other standard apparatus that will appear in future vessels
1914–1918	Germany uses hundreds of U-boats in combat in World War I
1915	A German U-boat sinks the passenger liner *Lusitania* on May 7, 1915, killing 1,195 passengers; the United States responds by entering World War I
1939	On May 23, Lieutenant Commander Swede Momsen and divers complete the first underwater submarine rescue, saving 33 survivors from the USS *Squalus*
1941–1945	During World War II, the U.S. Navy adopts German wolf-pack tactics in underwater combat against the Japanese in the Pacific; the war spurs advancements in submarine technology
1943	Jacques Cousteau invents self-contained underwater breathing apparatus (scuba)
1945	The cold war between the United States/NATO and the Soviet Union begins
1954	The United States launches the USS *Nautilus*, the world's first nuclear submarine

Chronology

1957	K-3, the first Soviet nuclear submarine, is launched
1959	The United States launches the USS *George Washington* (SSBN-598), the first nuclear-powered, fleet ballistic missile submarine.
1961	On July 4, the K-19, a ballistic-missile submarine, becomes the first Soviet nuclear vessel involved in an accident after a major leak develops in the reactor cooling system and irradiates the interior of the vessel; nine men die from radiation burns and poisoning
1963	USS *Thresher* (SSN-593) sinks with all hands on April 10 while conducting sea trials about 240 miles off the coast of Cape Cod, Massachusetts; 129 crewmen die
1968	On May 21, USS *Scorpion* (SSN-589) sinks with all hands; experts believe a torpedo explosion caused the accident, which kills 99 crewmen
1970	On April 12, 53 men die after Soviet submarine K-8 suffers a fire and sinks, while under tow, in the Bay of Biscay
1986	Soviet nuclear-powered–ballistic-missile submarine K-219 sinks near Bermuda on October 6 after a missile explosion; four men die in the accident, while the East Coast of the United States barely escapes radiation contamination
1989	Soviet nuclear-powered submarine K-278 sinks in the Norwegian Sea on April 7 during its maiden voyage; most of the crew is killed
2000	During an August 12 Russian naval exercise in the Barents Sea, the nuclear submarine *Kursk* suffers two explosions and plunges 350 feet to the sea bottom; the Russian navy begins rescue operations of *Kursk* the following day, as officials assure the public that the 118 trapped submariners are still alive; a week later, Norwegian divers open *Kursk*'s escape hatch to find no survivors
2001	On February 9, USS *Greeneville* (SSN-772) has an accidental collision with a Japanese high-school training ship, *Ehime Maru*; four Japanese students and five sailors are killed; in May, the media announces that the Dutch salvage firm Mammoet will raise *Kursk* by September 2001

Further Reading

Ballard, Robert D., and Malcolm McConnell. *Explorations: A Life of Underwater Adventure*. New York: Hyperion, 1995.

Clancy, Tom. *Submarine: A Guided Tour Inside a Nuclear Warship*. New York: Berkley Books, 1993.

Craven, John Piña. *The Silent War*. New York: Simon and Schuster, 2001.

Gray, Edwyn. *Few Survived*. London: Leo Cooper, 1996.

Hutchthausen, Peter, Igor Kurdin, and R. Alan White. *Hostile Waters*. New York: St. Martin's Press, 1997.

Kinder, Gary. *Ship of Gold in the Deep Blue Sea*. New York: Atlantic Monthly Press, 1998.

Maas, Peter. *The Terrible Hours*. New York: Harper Torch, 1999.

Sontag, Sherry, Christopher Drew, and Annette Lawrence Drew. *Blind Man's Bluff*. New York: Public Affairs, 1998.

Tyler, Patrick. *Running Critical*. New York: Harper and Row, 1986.

Verne, Jules. *20,000 Leagues Under the Sea*. New York: Tor Books, 1995.

Weir, Gary E. *Forged in War: The Naval-Industrial Complex and American Submarine Construction*. Washington, D.C.: Brassey's, 1998.

Index

Index

Index

Index

Picture Credits

CHRISTOPHER HIGGINS is an associate editor at Chelsea House. He lives in Philadelphia with his wife, Sima, and his new baby, Talia. He hopes that Talia grows up to become the first female captain of a Los Angeles–class nuclear attack submarine.

JILL McCAFFREY has served for four years as national chairman of the Armed Forces Emergency Services of the American Red Cross. Ms. McCaffrey also serves on the board of directors for Knollwood—the Army Distaff Hall. The former Jill Ann Faulkner, a Massachusetts native, is the wife of Barry R. McCaffrey, who served in President Bill Clinton's cabinet as director of the White House Office of National Drug Control Policy. The McCaffreys are the parents of three grown children: Sean, a major in the U.S. Army; Tara, an intensive care nurse and captain in the National Guard; and Amy, a seventh grade teacher. The McCaffreys also have two grandchildren, Michael and Jack.